Seven Simple Secrets

What the Best Teachers Know and Do

**Annette Breaux
and Todd Whitaker**

EYE ON EDUCATION
6 DEPOT WAY WEST, SUITE 106
LARCHMONT, NY 10538
(914) 833–0551
(914) 833–0761 fax
www.eyeoneducation.com

All poetry in this book is the original work of Annette Breaux.

Library of Congress Cataloging-in-Publication Data

Breaux, Annette L.
    Seven simple secrets : what the best teachers know and do / Annette Breaux and Todd Whitaker.
        p. cm.
    ISBN 1-59667-021-5
    1. Teaching—Handbooks, manuals, etc. 2. Classroom management—Handbooks, manuals, etc. I. Whitaker, Todd, 1959- II. Title.
    LB1025.3.B743 2006
    371.102—dc22

                                        2006000097

10 9 8 7 6 5 4 3 2 1

Editorial and production services provided by
Richard H. Adin Freelance Editorial Services
52 Oakwood Blvd., Poughkeepsie, NY 12603-4112
(845-471-3566)

Dedication

To all our fellow teachers, to whom we offer these seven secrets…

Seven Simple Secrets

Is a secret still a secret if you tell it to one other?
Because once you tell that other, she'll pass it to another
Who tells it to her best friend, who passes it around
And soon enough, this private thing has spread throughout the town
But sometimes it's a good thing to spread it far and wide
Some things are better known, than to silently have died

So look into your secret, and decide if you want it known
And if you do, you know how to, tell one and it's full blown

And so we've seven secrets to share with those who teach
We want to spread them wide and far, hoping they will reach
Every teacher everywhere, who wants to help, who truly cares
And soon we hope that everyone will know what they're about
You hold those secrets in your hands—now go on, let them out!

Annette Breaux and Todd Whitaker

About the Authors

Annette Breaux is one of the most entertaining and informative authors and speakers in education today. She leaves her audiences with practical techniques to implement in their classrooms immediately. Administrators agree that they see results from teachers the next day.

A former classroom teacher and curriculum coordinator and author of Louisiana FIRST, a statewide induction program for new teachers, Annette now serves as the teacher induction coordinator for Nicholls State University in Thibodaux, Louisiana. Annette has coauthored a book with Dr. Harry K. Wong on new teacher induction.

Her other writings include *101 Answers for New Teachers and Their Mentors; REAL Teachers, REAL Challenges, REAL Solutions; The Poetry of Annette Breaux: Tips and Poems for Teachers and Students;* and *10 Days to Maximum Teaching Success.*

Teachers who have read Annette's writings or heard Annette speak agree that they come away with user-friendly information, heartfelt inspiration, and a much-needed reminder that theirs is the most noble of all professions—teaching.

Dr. Todd Whitaker is a professor of educational leadership at Indiana State University in Terre Haute, Indiana. Prior to coming to Indiana, he taught at the middle and high school levels in Missouri. Following his teaching experience, he served as a middle school and high school principal for eight years. Dr. Whitaker also served as a middle school coordinator in Jefferson City, Missouri.

Dr. Whitaker's work has been published in the areas of teacher leadership, instructional improvement, change, leadership effectiveness, technology, and middle-level practices. His books include *Dealing with Difficult Teachers; Motivating & Inspiring Teachers; Dealing with Difficult Parents; Feeling Great!; Teaching Matters;* and *What Great Principals Do Differently.* His latest books are the number-one bestseller *What Great Teachers Do Differently* and *Great Quotes for Great Educators.* Dr. Whitaker is internationally recognized as an inspirational and distinguished speaker.

He is married to Beth, a former teacher and principal, who is an associate professor in the Elementary Education Department at Indiana State University. They are the parents of Katherine, Madeline, and Harrison.

Table of Contents

Foreword

Want to know a secret? The absolute best teachers are not the absolute best because they were born the absolute best. They're not the absolute best because they have the highest IQs. They were not the absolute best when they first started teaching. So why are they the absolute best? **They're the absolute best because they share something in common—seven simple secrets.** That's right—seven simple secrets that can and will change your life as a classroom teacher.

Though we do not suggest that just "anyone" can be a teacher, we do suggest that people who have been "called" to teach—those who really do want and have what it takes to make a difference, those who, we believe, constitute the majority of teachers in our classrooms today—can realistically become those teachers we consider the very best!

Thus, our intent in writing this book is to reveal the secrets of the most effective teachers to all of you who touch the lives of children every day. You hold the future in your hands, and now you hold the secrets to making that future a bright and prosperous one!

How to Use This Book

This book is divided into seven secrets shared by the very best teachers. Each secret is then divided into seven parts. The book is structured so that you may focus on one secret at a time or flip from page to page at random. Regardless of how you read the book—from cover to cover, one secret at a time, or allowing the wind to determine which page you read today—we guarantee that by implementing these seven simple secrets, you are on your way to becoming the most effective teacher you can possibly be!

What This Book Will Do for You

As educators, in our noble efforts to learn new techniques, to implement new strategies, to find the perfect program that will meet all of our students' varied needs, we often spread ourselves way too thin, run around in circles, meet ourselves coming and going, burn the candle at both ends, and eventually burn ourselves out. We end up resenting our jobs, bemoaning our work-loads, and wishing ourselves retired. Sound familiar?

The fact remains that regardless of what comes down the pike throughout your years of teaching, some things will never change—and in our haste and desperation, these are the very things, the simple things, that are often over-looked. Can good teaching really revolve around seven simple secrets? It can.

What you now hold in your hands are the seven simple secrets of the very best teachers. These secrets are simple and profound in their simplicity. They encompass no new programs and no late-breaking innovations, techniques, or strategies. Rather, they are seven simple secrets that the most effective teachers share—*period*. Implementing these secrets will change your life both in and out of the classroom. But most profoundly, they will enhance the lives of every student you teach.

To you, our fellow educators, we reveal these secrets in the hope that, one teacher at a time, we will be able to make a contribution to the children—our future.

Secret One

The Secret of Planning

The Rewards of Planning

Coaches go into every game with a very specific plan
And surgeons plan their surgeries and proceed with a steady hand
Attorneys defend their clients following much preparation
And players of chess only make a move after much deliberation
Travelers go on vacation with their maps and proper clothing
So why's it that some teachers speak of lesson plans with loathing?
The fact remains that failing to plan becomes a plan to fail
You're a ship without an anchor, a hammer without a nail
So plan your lessons every day
Stay on the path so you won't go astray
Know why you're teaching the things that you teach
And reap your rewards from the students you reach.

Part 1.
How to Have a Great Plan

The very best teachers know that if you want to *have* a great lesson, you need to *plan* a great lesson. It is truly that simple. But understand that planning takes time. However, if you teach with a well-planned lesson, then you can really enjoy your teaching. Now, does that mean that you will accomplish everything you intend to accomplish or that your plan will go off without a hitch? Of course not. Teaching is not an exact science, and that is why we need to plan so thoroughly.

The very first thing you will want to do, when you sit down to plan your lesson, is to center the entire plan around your *objective*—what it is you want the students to accomplish on that day. Let's say that today you will be teaching your students how to write a friendly letter. (The reason we chose this particular skill is that everyone, regardless of their content area, can relate to using this skill.) So your objective is that the students will be able to write a friendly letter, including all of the five parts—heading, greeting, body, closing, and signature. Now, the first thing you need to plan, of course, is how you will get your students to actually *want* to write a friendly letter. So you'll want to begin a discussion of some sort in which you ask them if they ever write letters to their friends. All students, at one time or another, have passed notes in class. Yes, you have their attention. You will, of course, lead the discussion beyond writing notes to their friends as you continue to discuss the friendly letter and its purpose. Then you may want to have a friendly letter already written to the class by you or another teacher or even the principal. Yes, this takes some preparation. It involves either writing the letter yourself or having someone else do it. But it's not difficult.

Let's say that you have the principal write a friendly letter to the class. (You may even choose to write the letter *for* the principal. It really doesn't matter, as long as you make the principal aware of what you wrote.) It is best to write the letter on chart paper or on an overhead transparency so that it is in an enlarged format, visible to all.

Now read the letter with the class, and then have them analyze each part with your guidance. As they analyze each part, have a student write the name of that part next to it. For instance, where it says, "Dear Class," the student would label it as the "greeting." You get the point. Bottom line? With your guidance, they will identify all of the parts of a friendly letter.

Now you'll want to *model* the skill for them. (By the way, modeling is one of the most important parts of teaching anything to anyone, yet it is often overlooked.) To model, simply write a letter to a friend of yours, either on the board, on chart paper, or on an overhead transparency. As you write, think aloud for the benefit of the students. You may even choose to allow them to guide you as you write. (Please take note that we have not yet, nor will we, give a definition of a friendly letter. Instead, we're pulling the information from the students. This is much more meaningful, and thus lasting.) After you've finished that, you might then plan to write a friendly letter, maybe in response to the principal, as a class. Either have a student write it on chart paper, or you can write it as they all participate.

Once you've actually taught and modeled the skill and then guided students through the skill, they should be ready to try the new skill on their own. So what should their assignment be? You guessed it. They will write their own friendly letters as you walk around and monitor for understanding. You may even choose to have them bring envelopes and stamps so that they can actually mail the letters. And now that that's done, you will always want to wrap up your lesson with a review to provide closure. The most effective teachers know that you never tell the students what they've learned. Instead, you have them tell and/or show you.

That's it. You've written a great plan! Yeah, but what if you have one or two students who don't spell all the words correctly in their friendly letters? Remember, the objective was to write a friendly letter including all of its parts. No one said anything about spelling everything correctly. While you're monitoring, simply help them with their spelling. And even if you didn't catch every misspelling, the bottom line is that they've accomplished the lesson's objective anyway! (Please don't misunderstand. We're not saying that spelling is not important. Rather, we're suggesting that you focus on the objective for that particular lesson on that particular day.)

In writing this book, we came up with a plan. First, we thought about our objective and decided that we wanted to share with everyone the secrets of the most effective teachers. Next, of course, we had to determine what the very best teachers have in common. We found seven things. Then we had to summarize, in a simple, easy-to-read format, those seven things that the most effective teachers know and do. We then decided to divide each secret into seven simple parts. After we had all of that in place, the book practically wrote itself. So it is in the classroom. If you have a really great plan, your lesson will practically teach itself!

Tips for Planning

The following are some simple tips for you to use when planning any lesson:

- Determine your objective.
- Decide how you will make the lesson interesting and inviting for your students.
- Be sure to make an effort to actively involve your students in every part of the lesson.
- Plan to state the lesson's purpose, relate the skill to students' real lives, teach and model the skill, practice the skill with them, have them try the new skill independently, and review. (See Secret 3, page 41.)
- Be sure to gather any necessary materials beforehand.
- Enjoy teaching your well-planned lesson!

We guarantee that any teacher who plans all lessons with activities such as the ones in the above plan and gives careful thought to every step of the lesson will see instant results from students.

> If you plan your lessons with careful attention and treat each one as a special invention, you're sure to see student success and retention, reducing your levels of stress and tension!

Part 2.
How to Overplan

The very best teachers, as part of their secret to successful planning, always overplan. Most, if not all, will admit that they learned this secret the hard way. As teachers, we can all relate to planning some lesson or activity that we thought would take a certain amount of time, only to realize that we were dead wrong. For instance, you are a teacher planning an activity, envisioning that it will take about 20 minutes. The activity turns out to take seven minutes. Now what? There are 13 minutes left to fill. What do you do? Unless you have overplanned, you resort to desperate measures. Yes, the ever-present, much-hated worksheet. And when that worksheet is finished, there's always another one waiting. Students, of course, are doing anything but completing the worksheet. Or, they finish the worksheet mindlessly, getting mostly wrong answers. During this time, the teacher is continually reminding students to get busy, to proofread their work, to stop talking, and so forth. And, of course, some students complete the worksheet within a couple of minutes, whereas others have not yet begun. So what do you do with the students who now have nothing to do? You resort to another desperate measure, like saying, "If you're finished, read your library book." Or better yet, "When you finish, put your head down and be quiet until everyone else is finished." Sound familiar? This frustrating, all-too-familiar scenario can be avoided by doing what the most effective teachers are doing—overplanning!

How do you overplan? You do just that. You plan more than you think you will need. However, a word of caution here: Don't just plan another of the same type of activity. This will bore students out of their minds. Instead, if one activity is successfully completed by your students, then it is time to take the newly acquired skill to the next level. Therefore, when overplanning, be sure to plan subsequent activities that are increasingly challenging for your students.

What's the downside of overplanning? There really isn't one. At worst, you will not get to do everything you have planned for that lesson. The most important thing is that you have actually managed to teach a new skill, successfully, to your students. And, as a bonus, you're left with more activities to use in future lessons. In the next section, you will learn a skill for managing your time that will also help you not to "overly" overplan!

When you're going on vacation, isn't it much better to have too many clothes than not enough? When flying to a destination, wouldn't any pilot prefer to have too much fuel than not enough? The same holds true in the classroom.

Part 3.
How to Manage Your Time

Even the very best teachers will admit that it's difficult to plan for a one-hour lesson and make sure that it actually takes an hour. It is even more difficult to plan for a 90-minute lesson and end within one or two minutes of 90 minutes. And even if you're overplanning, you don't want your 60-minute lesson to take only 30, so that you have to rely on 30 more minutes from your overplanning activities. Nor do you want your 60-minute lesson to take 90 minutes. So how is it that some teachers always manage to teach what they plan to teach in the amount of time that they actually plan to teach it? **The very best teachers have a secret. When planning their lessons, they plan in 5-minute segments.** In other words, a 60-minute lesson is broken into 12 five-minute segments. For instance, the introduction to the lesson is planned to last about five minutes. A brief discussion following the introduction may also take five minutes. Following that, the teacher may actually teach the new skill for one five-minute segment. The teacher may then actually take about 5 minutes to model the skill for the students. Following this, there may be two 5-minute activities in which the teacher practices the new skill with the students. Next, the teacher may put the students into cooperative groups for two five-minute segments. Following this, the students attempt the new skill independently for two five-minute segments while the teacher monitors for understanding. There are now two five-minute segments remaining. If students are having difficulty, another five-minute segment may be needed for reteaching or simply for more practice. If not, put that segment into the review activity, which may last for one or two five-minute segments, to be determined as the lesson progresses. That's it. That's a 60-minute lesson. And a good one at that!

When teachers plan this way, several things happen. It ensures that the lesson will continue to move and that the activities will be varied. This increases the likelihood of your holding the students' attention. It also ensures that you will not stay on one thing for too long—a fatal mistake made by many teachers. And finally, it keeps you within your time frame so that your lessons are well paced, almost always ending right on time!

Okay, but what if during your guided practice you notice that the students are not ready to try the skill independently after only one or two five-minute segments? Then you do what the best teachers do—you adjust.

You may, with some lessons, determine that your students will not be ready until the next day to attempt the new skill on their own. That's fine. Again, adjust as needed. But be constantly aware of each segment and how much time has passed. The easiest way to do this is by having a large clock on the classroom wall.

Have you ever wondered how it is that some speakers can manage to do a three-hour speech and end in exactly three hours? Or a one-hour keynote ending on the sixtieth minute? They, too, plan in five-minute segments. When planning, it's much easier to judge how much material you can cover in five minutes than to guess how much you can get into a full hour—or two or three.

So when planning your next lesson, try it. Oh, and by the way, if you have an activity that you believe will take only two minutes, don't stretch it to five for the sake of taking up five minutes. Just add the three minutes to your next segment, or plan an entire segment that will only take three minutes. You get the point.

A very important note: Please understand that we are not suggesting planning in five-minute segments to "eat up time." The best teachers utilize every minute of their time each day with effective teaching. They don't ever use "time fillers" or plan activities for the sake of how long they will last. They also don't move on to the next segment of the lesson if students are not grasping the concept, thinking, "Oh, well, my five minutes are up. Gotta move on!" It's just that they have "so much to teach," they want to make sure that every minute of their teaching time is utilized to the fullest! And thus they often plan in five-minute segments.

The fact is that students of any age, including adults, have difficulty staying focused on any one task for more than a few minutes anyway. And don't worry that it will take you longer to write your plans. It won't.

Wait, but what if you were planning on having students read the chapter for about 30 minutes? Well, let's think about that. Have you ever noticed that when you say, "Read the chapter," your students first spend about five minutes moaning and groaning? Then they usually get busy. But notice what happens after about five minutes. You begin redirecting them because most of them have gotten off task. They're spending their next five minutes staring into space or talking or fidgeting or drooling on the textbook. Aha! That's because they've lost their focus after about five minutes. So here's a technique for you. If you want them to read something in the chapter, or even the whole chapter, for that matter, who's to say it can't be meaningful, fun, and broken into five-minute segments? It can. Simply decide what you want them to read for on one page at a time, then tell them that you'll give them about two minutes to find out whatever it is you want them to find out. Then follow the reading with a meaningful discussion. Or better yet, divide the class into groups and have each group read a different section for a different purpose. Then come back together and have students discuss what they have learned. Any chapter in any subject can be fascinating to students if you approach it with a little creativity and a lot of activity.

> So teach in segments of five and see your classroom come alive!

Part 4.
How to Be Flexible

The very best teachers know that flexibility is a must in planning. Planning is simply that—planning what you think you will be able to accomplish with your students. But remember what they say about "the best-laid plans." In teaching, almost nothing ever goes exactly as planned. When writing your plans, you can't anticipate student questions, student levels of understanding of a particular new skill, unexpected interruptions, unanticipated fire drills, and so on. So you do the best you can—you plan, assuming that everything will be perfect, knowing, of course, that it won't.

Flexible people bend, but they don't break. They don't get as frustrated as others when something goes awry. They simply adapt. They don't feel like failures when something they plan does not work the way they had anticipated. They just adjust. If they don't accomplish everything they wanted to accomplish on any particular day or with any particular lesson, they carry it over to the next day's lesson.

Inflexible teachers walk around feeling like failures. They just never figure it out—teaching does not lend itself to perfectionism. Each lesson does not go off without a hitch. Signs on the door that say "Please Do Not Disturb" do not keep others from knocking. The PA system *will* be used at various inconvenient times throughout the day. Inflexible teachers actually spend a good part of any typical day complaining about the fact that nothing ever goes as planned. You've heard them. Do you recognize this? "Well, I actually counted the number of announcements today—eleven! When do they expect us to be able to teach with all these interruptions? And now they want us to turn in yet another piece of documentation. Oh, and how about the fire drill this morning? That was smart—right smack dab in the middle of math. By the time we got back to the classroom, the students had forgotten everything I'd been teaching them. And it took me 10 minutes just to settle them down before I could start teaching again." (Oh, and by the way, these teachers actually use class time to knock on their neighbors' doors to tell them these things.) They're allowing themselves to be miserable over things they can't control. And they're wasting precious teaching time sharing their miseries with others!

Yes, the very best teachers, in case you've never noticed, also tend to be the happiest teachers, the ones with the fewest ulcers, the ones who truly enjoy what they do, even when things don't always go the way they had planned. They've learned to focus on what they *can* control, not bemoan what they can't!

Remember:

- Plan well and thoroughly, but do not get bent out of shape if things don't go as planned.
- Steer clear of trying to make everything perfect.
- Accept the fact that any given school day involves many unexpected interruptions.
- There's *always* tomorrow!

Part 5.
How to Make Objectives Clear

Following a classroom observation, a teacher was asked, "What was the one thing you wanted your students to know or be able to do at the end of your lesson?" The observer, her principal, could not figure that out while observing the lesson. Before we get to the teacher's response, let's take a look at what the principal saw.

An Ineffective Lesson

The teacher began the lesson by saying, "Open your reading books to page 56." She then asked a student, "What is the title of the story?" Another was asked, "Who's the author?" Still another was asked, "Who's the illustrator?" Following these questions, the teacher said, "Now I want you to read the story, and when you've finished that, I want you to answer the story questions." The students reluctantly got busy reading while the teacher walked around the room trying to redirect students who were staring into space, talking, and so forth. Some students actually read the story—and they did so quite quickly. They then got busy on the questions and answered them equally as fast. Now these students were finished, and some of the students had not gotten past the first page or two of the story. The teacher then had the students who had finished the initial assignment summarize, in paragraph form, what they had just read. Needless to say, these students were not happy. Were they being punished for doing their work on time?

Okay, you get the picture. This went on for the entire class period, and some students never did finish reading the story and answering the questions. And then the bell rang.

So back to the principal's question (which was obviously a very legitimate one): "What was the one thing you wanted your students to know or be able to do at the end of your lesson?" And now for the teacher's answer: "Well, I wanted them to read the story and answer the questions at the end of the story to ensure their understanding."

Too many times, teachers just sort of drift around, get caught up in themes, etc., spending much time and effort not accomplishing a whole lot. It's not that they're lazy. On the contrary, some of these very same teachers spend exorbitant amounts of time planning lessons that don't really go anywhere. In this case, there was no real objective. Reading a story and answering questions are not objectives. They're activities! Further review of the textbook revealed that the objective was for the students to make, confirm, and reject predictions. You will notice, as the principal did, that nowhere during the lesson was this skill taught and modeled. Had it been, it could have made for an excellent lesson. We'll give you an example.

An Effective Lesson

An effective teacher is using the same story as the teacher above to teach the skill of making, confirming, and rejecting predictions. Notice the difference already, in that the teacher is not teaching a story but rather is using the story to teach a skill—that of making, confirming, and rejecting predictions. In her introduction, she asks the students about movies they have seen lately. They discuss what happens when seeing a movie for the first time—how we actually make predictions as to what will happen next and then confirm and reject those predictions as the movie progresses. This is then related to reading, with an explanation that the very same thing happens when we read; we begin making predictions as soon as we read the title, and we continually confirm and reject predictions as our reading of the story progresses. For the actual reading of the story, the teacher gives them "small bites" to read at a time. And as they read, they practice the new skill, stopping to discuss and recognize what's happening as they make, confirm, and reject their predictions. Do you see the difference? Instead of just saying, "Read the story and then answer the questions," the teacher guides the students as they practice a new skill. The teacher is using activities to teach a specific objective. But to do this, the teacher must be clear on what the objective for the lesson actually is!

The most effective teachers all have something in common: They know the difference between objectives and activities, and they plan their lessons based on one or two objectives. All activities, then, focus only on the objectives.

Also, in the most effective teachers' classrooms, the teachers actually *tell* the students, at the very beginning of the lesson, exactly what they'll be able to do at the end of this lesson. Remember, they're working toward mastery, not mystery.

Making objectives clear is vital to helping students learn. Be clear on where you're going with each lesson as you plan, and then plan only activities that will help to accomplish that objective.

When a surgeon goes into surgery to operate on you, don't you want him to have a plan and be clear on his objective? Plan each lesson as though you are a skilled surgeon. If you plan this way, students will not only survive, but they'll actually thrive!

Part 6.
How to Promote Activity

Do you know the 60/40 rule? It states that the students should be talking/doing 60 percent of the time, and the teacher should be talking/doing the remaining 40 percent. Now let's clarify. When we say talking/doing on the parts of the students, we do not mean discussing issues not related to the lesson or doing things not related to the lesson. And with regard to the teacher, the part that says the teacher should be talking/doing only 40 percent of the time does not mean that the other 60 percent he or she should be seated behind a desk! Okay, now that we have that straight, we will share with you that in far too many classrooms, the opposite is true. The teacher is doing most of the talking, and the students are expected to be quiet and listen, taking it all in, of course, with no activity beyond listening intently. Yeah, right. We all know better. **We know that whoever is doing the "doing" is doing the learning,** yet the practice of students "doing most of the doing" is not at all common. Well, it should be. In fact, it's one of the main things that sets the most effective teachers apart. They keep their students so busy that not only is there little, if any, time to misbehave, but there is, as a bonus, learning occurring!

So how do they do it? How do they manage to keep their students busy and actively, along with meaningfully, engaged throughout the entire lesson? The answer is simple: They *plan* for it. They plan their questioning so that students are constantly answering and thinking and analyzing and deducing and comparing. Bloom's Taxonomy, anyone? Let's look at a typical example. If you give your students, on Monday, of course, a list of 20 vocabulary words to define, you will hear and see the following:

- ◆ Moaning
- ◆ Groaning
- ◆ "Do we have to write the whole definition or just the first one?"
- ◆ "Do we have to write the part of speech?"
- ◆ "Why do we have to do this?"

And the list goes on. If this sounds familiar, we hope it isn't because it happens in your own classroom. But let's continue along that same line. The students, finally, do finish copying the definitions into their notebooks. Then you go over the definitions. They may even have to write a sentence with the words, and if they do, your most clever students even figure out ways around doing what you really wanted by writing sentences such as "I spelled the word *dandelion* correctly on my spelling test." They write the same, or at least a similar, sentence for each word and are finished in a few minutes. Technically, they have completed the assignment. But, of course, they have not really learned any new vocabulary. The most amazing thing is that, in many classrooms, students never really learn the vocabulary words, yet many actually ace their tests. Let's prove that point. Teachers, we all have to admit that if we have students memorize definitions for Friday's test, most of our students will at least pass that test. But what would happen if we gave the same test, unannounced, next week or the week after? Most would do poorly on the test, proving the point that we have not actually taught and the students have not actually learned the new vocabulary.

So what do the most effective teachers do? They "can" the lists.

"Can" the Lists!

On Monday you gave me 20 words for Friday's vocabulary test
I wrote them five times every night and I studied my very best
On Friday, I was well prepared to spit them back to you
I got them all, word for word, as I was expected to do
But I have a confession to make to you—despite the grade I earned
Those words have left my memory now; no vocabulary have I learned
You see, I never used the words or spoke them in conversation
So I guess we both just wasted our time—what an awful revelation!
So next time, leave the lists alone; make me use the words
If you don't, then I'll soon lose them; they'll fly away like birds
I want to keep whatever I learn; I want to deserve the grade I earn
I want to be smart and witty and wise, but wisdom doesn't come when I memorize!
I really do want to learn, you know, so "can" the lists and watch me grow!

Note that, like in the poem above, the most effective teachers *do* teach vocabulary. They don't, however, overwhelm students with too many words at a time. And they make their students *use* the words as opposed to simply memorizing the definitions.

And, of course, beyond vocabulary, the most effective teachers don't rely much on having students memorize notes, complete copious amounts of worksheets, read long and boring chapters independently, answer the questions at the ends of the chapters, and so on. Instead, they get their students involved in, for example, using the content, figuring out answers to problems, working cooperatively, presenting their findings to their classmates, and explaining to the teacher how they arrived at various conclusions.

Their classrooms are always humming with activity, and students are generally successful. There is never a dull moment in the classrooms of the most effective teachers, and no two days look the same. Students actually walk out of these classrooms anxious to return the next day!

> So have a proclivity to plan for activity, and learning will be brewing as your students do the doing.

Part 7.
How to Be Proactive

Time and again, research has continued to show what we continue to observe—the most effective teachers know the secret of being *proactive*. Let's simplify that term. **Being proactive means anticipating typical problems and warding them off before they have a chance to take place.** It means staying a step ahead of your students. Often, teachers wait for students to misbehave, and then they react with a punishment, a warning, a loss of control, and so forth. Here's a typical example. Two teachers were attempting to use cooperative grouping for the first time with their seventh graders. Follow us into their classrooms.

Ms. Reactive

Ms. Reactive announced to the class that they would be working in groups. However, she warned them, if they abused this privilege, they would lose this privilege. She then said, "I'm going to announce the names of the people in each group." And thus the chaos began. She named the first four people for group one, and one student sighed and said that he did not want to be in so-and-so's group. An angry glare from the teacher followed. As she announced the rest of the groups, much of the same continued. Students began asking to be moved to other groups. The teacher then reacted by saying, "If I hear one more word, you can forget the whole thing." Then, once the students were told to move into their groups, the chaos continued. Some moved quickly, others rammed their desks into other desks, and a few began arguing with their new group members immediately. Again the teacher said, "If I hear one more word, that's it." It gets worse, but we'll spare you the details. Needless to say, in less than 10 minutes, the students were back in rows, never to work in groups again in the classroom of Ms. Reactive.

Now on to Ms. Proactive's classroom. (Notice the psychology she used. It's beautiful!)

Ms. Proactive

Ms. Proactive enthusiastically announced to the class that because of their outstanding potential, she was going to allow them to begin working in cooperative groups from time to time. "But," she announced, "please don't worry about a thing. I'll walk you through the process, step by step, and I'll get you ready to be completely successful and stress-free when working in your groups." The students were already smiling. "Now," she said, "do you remember last year when you were much younger?" Heads began nodding in agreement. "Well, last year, I'm not sure that you would have had the maturity that it takes to do the kinds of things that we'll be doing in groups this year. But this year, I know you're ready. In a little while, I'm going to announce the people in each group. But first, think back to last year. As mere sixth graders, what would you have been tempted to do or say if I had called your name and put you in a group with someone who possibly was not your very best friend?" Hands went up, and several students shared that they might have complained aloud or pouted. "Yes," said Ms. Proactive, "you very well may have done that. But how would you feel if classmates complained because they did not want you in their group?" The students freely discussed the fact that they would have been upset by this. "So," said Ms. Proactive, "I just want to thank you in advance for being so grown-up and realizing that even though everyone in the world, or even in this classroom, will not be your best friend, we can all learn to work cooperatively, which, of course, is a sign of true maturity."

She then announced the names of students in each group, and there were no complaints whatsoever. Imagine that! Ms. Proactive then explained and demonstrated the procedure that they would use to get into their groups. More discussion followed, and they then began to practice getting into groups. Again, without a hitch! And finally, she explained that each person in the group would be given a job. These jobs would change with each new activity. Again, much explanation, much discussion, and much practice *before* the actual first try. To make a long story short, Ms. Proactive's class continued to work in cooperative groups for the rest of the year.

Ms. Proactive had been just that—proactive. She had anticipated the fact that children will be children, and thus they must be told how to get along, how to get into their groups, exactly what to do once they are in their groups, how to get out of their groups, and so forth. And thus she planned accordingly, avoiding all of the problems faced in the classroom of Ms. Reactive. She set them up for success! She planned the social-skills aspect, the expectations aspect, and the organizational aspect before she even mentioned to the students that they would be working in groups. At all times, she remained a step ahead of them.

And therein lies the difference between proactive and reactive teachers. Proactive teachers *act.* Reactive teachers *react.* And by the way, it's easy to be proactive. You just think like a child. Because all of us *were* children, it's easy. If you can think like a child, then you will know how to anticipate your students' actions and responses to just about any situation. Once you've anticipated that, you move into adult mode and outsmart them!

> It's fun, we won't deny it, and you'll like it if you try it!

Secret One—Chapter Summary

In planning, remember the following:
- If you want to have a great lesson, you have to have a great plan.
- Plan your entire lesson around very clear and specific objectives.
- Plan lessons that will interest and involve your students.
- Remember the 60/40 rule.
- Always overplan.
- Manage your time by planning in five-minute segments.
- Remain flexible and adapt when necessary.
- Focus on what you *can* control. Don't bemoan what you can't.
- Remember that an objective is a very specific goal—what you plan on accomplishing by the end of the lesson. An activity is one of many ways of reaching that goal.
- Take action to avoid reaction!

Secret Two

The Secret of Classroom Management

Who's in Charge?

She was a classroom teacher and she didn't use much prudence

She tried to fit in by acting and by dressing like her students

When asked just why she did this, she said, "They'll think I'm cool"

And so they did, but not one kid respected her at school

And she couldn't understand just what could have gone awry

They liked her but didn't respect her. Each day, big tears she'd cry

No learning in her classroom, just foolishness all day long

She tried to undo the mess she'd wrought, the tangle of things gone wrong

It changed the day that she stopped adding injury to insult

The day she finally realized that she was the adult

And from that day she donned a most professional attire

She set clear rules and procedures—her classroom hummed like a choir

Her enthusiasm was contagious and her students were infected

And she became one of the rare ones that every child loved and respected.

Part 1.
What an Effective Teacher's Classroom Looks Like

Remarkably, in our observations, we found that the most effective teachers' classrooms all looked uncannily similar. And, of course, the same can be said for the less effective teachers—their classrooms all looked uncannily similar. It seemed, also, that no matter where we went, the students all acted the same in the classrooms of the most effective teachers. And yes, no matter where we went, the students all acted the same in the classrooms of the less effective teachers. We are, of course, speaking in generalities here.

Let's take a look inside the **less effective teachers' classrooms** first. Here is what they all had in common:

- The classroom looked disorganized. There was random "stuff" everywhere.
- Lessons lacked enthusiasm and excitement on the part of the teacher and, consequentially, among the students.
- The teacher did most of the talking, and the students did little listening.
- There was little, if any, evidence of structured routines and procedures.
- There were lots of teacher warnings for student misbehavior.
- There were numerous interruptions of the lesson for the teacher to try to reestablish control. (Note: We use the word reestablish lightly, as the fact is that control was never fully established in the first place.)
- The teacher was reactive.
- Lesson plans were vague and often confusing.
- A clear objective was usually nonexistent.
- There was little teacher movement around the room. The teacher generally stayed at the front of the room. Guess where most of the behavior problems occurred!
- There was an overuse of worksheet and independent textbook activities.
- The punishment for any given infraction lacked consistency. The severity of the punishment was usually in direct proportion to the teacher's anxiety level.

- The teacher openly showed frustration.
- The lessons were usually "one size fits all." Unfortunately, most fit none.
- There was little, if any, positive reinforcement.
- The teacher rarely smiled. In fact, in almost all cases, the teacher appeared to dislike teaching.

We could go on and on, but we think we've made the point. So now for the good news. Here's what we saw in the classrooms of **the most effective teachers:** (At the risk of insulting your intelligence, we'll state this anyway: The list below is the exact opposite of the list above.)

- The classroom looked organized. There was a place for everything, and everything was in its place.
- Lessons were filled with enthusiasm and excitement on the part of the teacher, and, consequentially, among the students.
- The students did most of the talking and the doing, prompted by the teacher's questioning and guidance.
- Routines and procedures were evident. Students knew exactly what was expected of them.
- There were no teacher warnings for student misbehavior. If a rule was broken, there was a consistent consequence.
- There were almost no interruptions of the lesson for the purpose of reestablishing control.
- The teacher was proactive.
- Lesson plans were well written. Any teacher could have picked up the plans and taught from them, knowing exactly what to do.
- The objective of the lesson was always clearly established for the students. There was no doubt in their minds what they were learning and why they were learning it.
- There was constant teacher movement around the room. Guess what happened to behavior problems! They were almost nonexistent.
- There was little dependence on worksheet and independent textbook activities. Lessons were inviting and exciting, and students remained actively engaged in meaningful activities.
- The punishment for any given infraction was consistent.
- The teacher almost never openly showed frustration. Even in the rare case of misbehavior, the problem was handled seriously but calmly. The teacher never appeared to be anything but in control.

- The lessons' activities were varied to meet the needs of all learners.
- There was constant positive reinforcement.
- The teacher often smiled and always appeared to actually love teaching.

So it's really quite simple. You now have a blueprint for what an effective teacher's classroom looks like. Make your room look like the classrooms of the most effective teachers and see what happens. Go ahead. You can do this.

Just try our blueprint on for size, and get your teaching organized. Management is the key to success. Just do it, and be at your best! For an organized teacher is a happier one than one who has let things come undone.

Part 2.
The Difference Between Rules and Procedures

Let's start out by simplifying. A *rule* is not the same as a *procedure*. **A rule is something that regulates a serious student misbehavior** such that if it's broken, there must be a consequence *every time.* **A procedure is simply a way that you expect something to be done**—the same way, every time it's done.

So what's the big deal? The big deal is that many teachers confuse the two and therefore create unnecessary problems and confusion. Here's one of the most obvious that we discovered in our observations: We found that many teachers have 10 or more rules posted in their classrooms. And none of these are consistently enforced. The biggest mistake is this: Many teachers post a rule stating that the students will not talk out of turn. But the fact is that we were unable to find even *one* teacher who actually punished every student who talked out of turn. Instead, we observed teachers who would see students talking, put a finger to their lips to remind students to be quiet, tell them they were getting too loud, remind them they were supposed to raise their hands, or, eventually, in desperation, when things got really out of hand, say, "The next person who talks will be punished!" When the next student eventually talked, he was punished, and he or she usually rebelled on the premise that "Everyone else was talking. Why are you punishing only me?" So what went wrong? What went wrong was that talking out of turn was not a rule; rather, it was a procedure mistakenly posted as a rule because the teacher was not aware of the difference between rules and procedures. Again, a rule is designed to regulate serious misbehaviors. Therefore, if it's broken, there must be a consequence every time.

So what did we find in the classrooms of the most effective teachers? Interestingly, the most effective teachers had very few rules and lots of procedures. In talking to these teachers, we noted that they were very clear on the difference between the two. They knew that procedures were simply consistent ways of doing things. Here's an example:

Procedure: We agree that we will raise our hands before speaking.

Rule: We agree that we will never hit another student.

We also noted that both the rules and procedures were stated in positive terms. To say "We agree..." is much more optimistic than saying "You will not..." Little things make big differences. (In Part 3, page 28, we show you how to establish rules and procedures.)

In the classrooms of the most effective teachers, there were procedures for practically everything, from walking into the room, to sharpening pencils, to taking roll, to passing in papers, to talking, to throwing away trash, and so on. Students knew exactly what was expected of them, and they generally followed the procedures. Regarding rules, there were only a handful, but they were clearly posted, along with the consequences for not following them. Again, there was no question as to what *not* to do and what would happen if a rule was broken. Rules, too, were generally followed by the students.

Conversely, **in the classrooms of the less effective teachers, there was a general lack of consistency** in doling out consequences and, as stated earlier, there was no clear distinction between rules and procedures. It was painfully obvious that no students knew exactly what was expected of them, as there were no clearly defined, consistent ways of doing things. Chaos often resulted.

We also found, in observing the most effective teachers, that because procedures were clearly established, there were very few discipline problems. The rules, of course, were reserved for only the serious infractions, and those rarely occurred. If they did, however, the consequences were immediate. No questions asked!

Okay, now to the burning question: What do you do, if there are no real consequences, when a student does not follow a procedure? Do you just look the other way when a student continually talks out of turn? If you do, won't there be chaos? How will you reestablish control if you're not punishing them when they keep doing things the wrong way? Good questions. And now for the good answers.

Neither we nor the most effective teachers advocate ignoring students when they do not follow procedures. In fact, you must do the opposite. Notice everything immediately, and deal with it promptly. In observing the most effective teachers, we noticed, first, that when a procedure was established, it was rehearsed over and over and over again. And then, when a student "forgot" the procedure, he was gently reminded. If more than one student forgot the procedure, the procedure was quickly practiced with the whole class. The teacher did not get bent out of shape. Instead, the teacher practiced the procedure with the students, always pretending to assume that the students had simply forgotten and therefore needed a little more practice. There were no warnings, empty threats, or punishments. These practice sessions were quick and effective.

But what about the student who is a chronic talker, the one who continues to talk out of turn even when he or she has been reminded and has practiced and practiced? Here's what we found. We found that the most effective teachers first began by reminding the student about the procedure. If that did not work, they did not continue to practice the procedure with the whole class, as this would waste time and insult those who continued to follow the procedure. Instead, they began by having a private conversation with the student who was the chronic talker. The student was reminded about the procedure, and the expectation was set that he would now follow the procedure. If that did not work, the teacher began to hold private practice sessions, usually at recess or right after class, with the student. (And by the way, this practice was used with and, not surprisingly, worked with students of all ages.) Now, how long do you think it would take to practice being quiet in a private session with your teacher? Not very. These sessions lasted only a minute or two, and the student was told that the teacher would be happy to give the student as much practice as necessary to help him or her become proficient in the procedure. Oh, the wonders of psychology!

But just in case, let's tackle the most extreme case. If all of the above had been tried and the student continued to be a chronic talker, then that procedure eventually became a rule for that one student. Yes, from that point forward, if the student spoke out of turn, there was a consequence. But this approach was used only as a last resort, and its occurrence was rare.

So let's recap. A rule is reserved for the most serious offense, and it has a definite consequence. Just about everything else falls into the category of procedure. The procedure is taught and practiced and then practiced some more. Consistency is the key!

The bottom line is that in the classrooms of the most effective teachers, rules are few and procedures are plenty. Everyone knows what to do and how to do it. If a student chooses to break a rule, there is a definite, preestablished consequence. If a procedure is not followed, the student is reminded and the procedure is practiced again.

If you want good discipline, be insistent that rules and procedures are clear and consistent.

Part 3.
How to Establish Rules and Procedures

Now that you're clear on the difference between rules and procedures, let's take a look at how the most effective teachers actually go about establishing these. We'll start with the rules.

The most effective teachers have very few rules, anywhere from three to five. Here are the steps they take to establish them:

Step 1. Decide what the rules will be. For instance, one rule might be that the students must enter the room before the tardy bell. Usually, this is a schoolwide rule, as we cannot have students roaming the campus when they are supposed to be in class. (We'll walk you through all of the steps, as once you understand the process, you'll be able to apply it to any rule you choose to establish in your own classroom.)

Step 2. Determine what the consequence will be if a student chooses to break a rule. For instance, if a student does not arrive for class before the tardy bell, then he or she must report to the office for a tardy slip. An exception, of course, would be that if another teacher or administrator is responsible for the student's tardiness, then the student must acquire a note from that person before entering your classroom. You may then decide that if a student has two tardy offenses (not including those with valid excuses from other teachers or administrators), then parents are notified. If the offenses become chronic, the administrator will determine the next step. Please note that this is a rule because it is a potentially serious offense. You simply cannot have students roaming the halls or the school grounds freely when they are supposed to be in your classroom.

Step 3. The most effective teachers begin by holding a discussion with students about rules and their purposes. The teacher, of course, has already established what the rules will be, but instead of just handing out the rules or announcing them in any kind of threatening way, he or she, through a discussion, actually gets the students to discuss the importance of the rule. The teacher, through carefully guided questions, leads the students into thinking they actually came up with the rule. Typical questions and conversation for the tardy rule might include: "I know that we all want to do our best and learn as much as we possibly can this year, and I promise you that I'll do my best to make sure that that happens. You see, I care about each of you, and I want to be the best teacher I can possibly be. Now, I don't think we need a lot of rules. Do you?" The students always agree that they do not want lots of rules. The teacher then may say something like, "Well, let's try to agree on only three rules. As I said, I want you to learn as much as possible this year. Do you think that, for you to learn, it might be important that you're actually here?" The students will agree. They always do. Of course, that doesn't mean that one little "smarty" might not say he or she can learn better when not present. Either choose to ignore that and move on with the discussion, or be even "smartier" (we know that's not a word, but it should be) and say something like, "I had another student who felt that way one year, so we tried it and it didn't work. So thank goodness the research saved you from having to try that one out." And then move on. Then say something like, "So we've agreed that we've got to get to class on time. That will make an excellent rule." Note that you may also choose to discuss the fact that you, as the teacher, are responsible for them once the bell rings. So, for legal reasons, you want all of your students safe and secure with you from bell to bell. Again, the way you state this will determine the degree to which they accept it.

Now, if there is a schoolwide tardy policy, tell the students that you follow all school rules, and the school rule states, for example, that if they do not arrive for class on time, they must report to the office for a tardy slip. Whatever the consequence is, just be sure that it is clearly understood by the students.

Step 4. Have the students help with the wording of the rule. Use clear language, and state that language in the most positive way possible. For instance, "We agree that we will be in class before the tardy bell."

Step 5. Post the rules, along with the consequences for not following them.

Step 6. Send parents a copy of the rules and consequences.

Step 7. Be consistent in enforcing the rules.

That's it! But the fact remains that less effective teachers make two common mistakes. First, they have too many rules, often confused with procedures, and second, they do not enforce the rules consistently.

And now for the procedures. Before we show you how the most effective teachers establish those, we'll provide you with a general list (but not an all-inclusive one) **of the types of things that typically require procedures:**

- How to walk into the room
- What to do when you enter the room
- How to pass in papers
- What to do when you need a pencil sharpened
- How to ask for permission to speak
- How to get into groups
- What to do when you're in your groups
- How to get out of groups
- How to walk to lunch
- How to exit the classroom
- What to do in case of a fire drill
- What to do when you have paper to throw away
- What to do when you're taking a test

And, of course, the list goes on, because many things require procedures.

It is important to note that the most effective teachers do not establish all procedures on the first day of class. Rather, they determine the most important procedures and establish those first. During the first week of class, they gradually establish a few more each day. It is also important to know that you may establish new procedures later in the year as the need arises.

The following is **the process that the most effective teachers use when establishing procedures:**

Step 1. State the procedure and the importance of following it.

Step 2. Model the procedure for the students. Show them exactly how you want it done.

Step 3. Practice the procedure with the students.

Step 4. Remind the students about the procedure right before they are expected to follow it. Then praise them often, throughout the year, when they do follow it.

Step 5. If a student does not follow the procedure, provide more practice. (Remember that in the previous section we explained how to do that.)

Step 6. Remain consistent with the procedures. If your procedure is that you will raise your hand when you need the students' attention, don't resort to asking them to get quiet, begging them to listen, reminding them that they're not listening, flicking the lights on and off, and so forth.

> Remember: A rule has a consequence; a procedure does not. And if you're consistent, good discipline you've got!

Part 4. What to Do if Your Students "Don't"

At the risk of being redundant, we will share with you a few techniques used by the most effective teachers when their students do not follow the rules and/or procedures. But we will begin by sharing what not to do if your students do not follow the rules and/or procedures.

Let's start with **a student not following a rule.**

What *not* to do:

- Warn the student to follow the rule after he or she has already broken it
- Allow yourself to lose control because the student has chosen to break the rule
- Allow your anger and/or frustration level to determine the consequence
- Make up the rules as you go

What *to* do:

- Announce to the student that because he or she chose to break the rule, he or she must now suffer the consequence
- Be consistent with your rules and consequences
- Ensure that the rules are always posted, along with the consequences, and that these rules and consequences were discussed *before* any student had a chance to break the rules

And now for **a student who does not follow a procedure:**

What *not* to do:

- Beg and plead
- Resort to empty threats
- Punish the student for not following a procedure
- Ignore the fact that the student is not following the procedure
- Be inconsistent with procedures

What *to* do:

- Remind the student, or have the student remind you, of the procedure
- Practice the procedure with the student
- Hold private practice sessions (as discussed in the previous section) if necessary

Secret 2. Part 4.

- Make the procedure a rule for that particular student if the problem is chronic (as discussed in the previous section)

Following are examples of both ineffective and effective ways that two teachers handled the same situation.

Scenario: The class was walking to lunch, and a student was not following the procedure. (The procedure was that the students would walk to lunch in single file without talking.) Though the student remained in line, he was talking.

Ineffective: The teacher ignored the talking until it got rather loud. The teacher then told the student to stop talking and continued walking to lunch with the class. The student, of course, began talking again once the teacher turned away. Then several other students began talking. The teacher told another student to stop talking, and he said, "I wasn't the only one." The teacher then said, "The next person who talks is going straight to the office!" Within seconds, the lucky student was on his way.

Note that in the above situation, the teacher was inconsistent. First, she ignored the fact that a student was not following the procedure. This, of course, only caused the problem to worsen. When the talking continued, the teacher gave a warning. Soon, the problem was out of hand. Then the teacher resorted to threats. And finally, the procedure became a rule because the teacher became frustrated.

Effective: In this situation, the second the student began talking, the teacher stopped and said to the student, "Oh, did you forget? What's the procedure for walking to lunch?" (Please note that there was not one hint of sarcasm or frustration in the teacher's voice. Rather, she acted as though she really believed that the student had simply forgotten the procedure.) And guess what happened? The student immediately stopped talking. Problem solved, right? Usually, but not in this case. Again, just a few moments later, the student talked again. This time, the teacher took the student aside and said, in a most sincere tone, "Look, I can see you're having trouble remembering the procedure. Don't worry about it. I forget things, too. But I know how embarrassing it can be to forget so often in front of your peers, so I'm going to do something for you. As soon as everyone is situated in the lunchroom, I'm going to give up some of my own lunch time to practice with you. Don't worry. I don't mind. I just want to help you to get really good at this procedure so that you won't be embarrassed in front of your peers anymore." Again, no sarcasm. The teacher made it sound as though she was doing the student a favor rather than punishing him. So, as soon as everyone was situated, the teacher asked another teacher to watch her class and she and the student went out for a private practice session. And guess what! The student got it right on the first try. So the teacher then asked, "Do you think we need to practice one more time, because even though I'm hungry, I'm willing to do that for you." The student, of course, declined the offer, assuring the teacher that he now knew the procedure. And the best part is that the student continued to follow the procedure the next day and the next.

Note that in the above situation, the teacher did two things. First, she was clear on what the procedure was, and when the student did not follow it, she addressed it immediately. Second, when the student did not follow the procedure yet again, the teacher used some good old psychology to make sure that the problem would not occur again. She did not lose her temper. Instead, she acted as though she was actually sacrificing her own lunch time because she cared so much about the student's "obvious embarrassment" in front of his peers. It's not rocket science! It's called outsmarting your students.

When your students don't follow your rules and/or procedures, simply do what the most effective teachers do: Be clear when establishing your rules and procedures, and then be consistent in holding your students accountable.

> Regarding rules and procedures, simply decide how you're going to do it, and then stick to it!

Part 5. Bell-to-Bell Teaching

A teacher told her students one day, "We have two minutes until the bell rings. If you can be quiet, I will not give you anything else to do." Can you guess what happened? Do you think the students actually remained quiet? Of course they didn't. The teacher then got upset and even told a coworker, "I tried to be nice and give them a break, but they took advantage. They're so inappreciative. Kids today!"

What the teacher later realized, as she relayed the story to us, was that it wasn't the students at all. And it wasn't the teacher. And it wasn't that you just can't be nice. Instead, it was the fact that the students had, for two minutes, nothing to do. In case you have not yet figured it out, the fact is that if you give students (of any age) nothing to do, they will find something to do every time.

Moral of the story? Do what the most effective teachers do: Don't ever give your students "nothing" to do. Keep them busy at all times. It's called teaching from bell to bell. **The busier students are, the less time they have to misbehave.** And let's also not forget the fact that **the busier students remain, the better their achievement!**

Students with idle time are either sleeping or misbehaving. Now, please understand that when we say to keep them busy, we do not mean you should feed them packets of worksheets to complete or endless chapters to read or a list of vocabulary words to define. During these types of activities, students get bored because they just don't see the point in the assignment. Neither do we, but that's for another chapter. So when students do not see work as meaningful, they switch into that idle mode and opt for either sleeping or misbehaving. (The latter seems to be the behavior of choice!)

Teaching from bell to bell means that you actively engage your students in *meaningful* activities from bell to bell. When the bell rings to signify the end of the class period and your students say, "Already?" then you know that you've succeeded. The students have been so engaged that the time has flown by. You should feel the same way.

We will take the liberty of changing the old adage "Time flies when you're having fun" to "Time flies when you're meaningfully engaged."

> So keep them engaged all the day, leaving no time for mischievous play. Learning will soar and knowledge will grow, and the class is over before you know!

Part 6. How to Discipline Proactively

What does it look like when a student is about to misbehave? Believe it or not, even the least effective teachers can answer this question. Parents know the answer, teachers know the answer, and anyone who has ever been a child knows the answer to this question. However, what sets the best teachers apart from the rest is the fact that they don't "wait" for the misbehavior to happen. **Less effective teachers run around putting out fires, whereas the most effective teachers practice fire prevention.**

It is a fact that the best teachers have the fewest discipline problems. And contrary to the beliefs of less effective teachers, it is not because they get the best students every year. Rather, it is because they implement the seven secrets we have addressed in this book. Their classrooms are well managed, their lessons are well planned, their demeanors are positive, they are consistent in implementing rules and procedures, they actively involve students in their lessons, they love teaching, they remain professional in any situation, they teach from bell to bell, and they enjoy positive relationships with their students.

Are we oversimplifying? Absolutely not. The very best teachers take the necessary measures to prevent children from misbehaving. Does that mean that no child ever misbehaves in their classrooms? No. However, when a child occasionally does misbehave, there is a structured plan in place for dealing with it. And dealing with problems swiftly, professionally, and consistently becomes a proactive measure for preventing future discipline problems.

Classroom Scenario

(From *REAL Teachers, REAL Challenges, REAL Solutions*, Breaux and Breaux, Eye On Education, 2004.)

We will take a look into the classrooms of two teachers, Ms. Proactive and Ms. Reactive. It is the first week of school. Both are teaching the same students. Both face the challenges of dealing with off-task behavior. One deals with the challenges effectively and nips them in the bud. The other deals with the same challenges ineffectively and allows them to escalate into full-blown problems. Follow us first into the classroom of Ms. P.

Ms. Proactive

Ms. P is holding a discussion with her class. During the discussion, she notices that Timothy is far away inside of a daydream. She continues the discussion and moves closer to Timothy. There is no change in her tone, no change in the manner in which the discussion is being held. She simply moves closer to Timothy. As she reaches his desk, she stands there, still continuing with the discussion. Timothy immediately snaps out of his daydream and joins the world of the classroom. He is back on task. The discussion continues, and Ms. P notices that Susan is attempting to get the attention of Natasha so that she can pass along a note. Ms. P stops the discussion and says, "Susan." Susan thinks that she is busted, and she stops dead in her tracks. Ms. P simply smiles and says, "Remind me that I have to tell you something before you leave today. I'm afraid I'll forget, so please remind me if I do." Susan nods and breathes a sigh of relief. She then puts the note away. Has she been busted? She's not sure, but she's definitely back on task. And by the way, Ms. P has no idea what she's going to tell Susan, as it was just a clever way of getting her back on task. But she's a teacher. She'll think of something!

Following the discussion, students spend a few minutes on a written assignment. Ms. P notices that Fred is doing nothing. Everyone else is working, but Fred is simply sitting in his desk, staring into space. Ms. P walks over to Fred and quietly says, "I can tell you're having trouble getting started. Do you need some help? I'll be happy to help you if you're stuck." It becomes evident that the student does not understand the assignment, so Ms. P does some simple remediation. Fred then gets busy.

Some time later, the bell rings, signaling the end of the period. The students now walk next door to the classroom of Ms. R. Same students, same challenges, different results. Let's see why things go awry.

Ms. Reactive

The class has begun, and Ms. R is holding a discussion with the students. Timothy did not get a chance to finish his daydream in Ms. P's class, so he revisits it in Ms. R's class. Noticing that Timothy is far away, Ms. R stops the discussion and stares at Timothy. A silence falls upon the class, and Timothy is awakened by the silence only to feel the heat of Ms. R's glare. Ms. R then says, in a tone that more than hints at sarcasm, "Well, Timothy, I'm so glad that you decided to join us." Timothy gets defensive and insists that he was paying attention. Determined to prove herself right, Ms. R then proceeds to question him about what has just been discussed. Timothy, of course, cannot come up with the correct answers. This makes him angrier, and a power struggle ensues. He is determined now to seek revenge. Maybe today, maybe later, but he'll get her for embarrassing him in front of his peers. He pouts for the remainder of the class period, completely removed from anything that is going on in class. As the discussion continues, Susan remembers that she still has the note for Natasha. She attempts to get Natasha's attention, holding the note in her hand. Ms. R marches straight to Susan and pulls the note from her hands. Again, another power struggle ensues. Susan decides to talk to Timothy after class. Maybe they can commiserate and cooperate in their master plan to get back at Ms. R. Susan, too, has been lost for the remainder of class period.

Later, as students complete a task at their desks, Fred, as is his tendency, is doing nothing. Ms. R tells him in no uncertain terms that he had better get busy if he wants to avoid after-school detention. Fred continues to do nothing. She warns him again, and he says he doesn't understand what he's supposed to do. Ms. R continues to threaten him, and soon he is sent to the office for willful disobedience. Susan adds his name to the list for commiseration and cooperation. There's power in numbers!

Bottom Line

You can deal with discipline challenges in a proactive manner or in a reactive manner. If you deal with them in a proactive manner, by nipping them in the bud before they escalate into real problems, your approaches will be effective. If you deal with them in a reactive manner, by acting out of emotions, taking the behaviors personally, and daring students to continue the behaviors, your approaches will be ineffective.

Ms. P deals with the challenges effectively. As a result, she gets the three off-task students back on task. At the same time, she maintains their dignity. She's off to a great start because she knows how to keep students on task. Thus, her students will achieve, and that will make for a wonderful and productive school year!

Ms. R deals with the challenges ineffectively. As a result, she loses the three off-task students. She does this by compromising their dignity and thus inviting revenge. This is only the first week of school. Both she and her students have entered the boxing ring. The students are determined to be victorious, hoping for a knockout before the 12th round! Ding!

> Remember, if you can prevent the fire, you'll never use the fire extinguisher!

Part 7. How *Not* to Be a Screamer

Though we do not suggest that you do the following, imagine that you went into a school where you knew no one, you assembled all the students in the auditorium, and you asked them, "Who are the 'screamers' on the faculty?" Could the students answer this question? You bet they could—and with 100 percent accuracy!

The fact is that, in any school, the students know who the screamers are; the parents know, and the principal knows. The only ones oblivious to their dubious reputations are the screamers themselves. They have no idea just how unprofessional their actions make them appear to others. If they did, they would not be screaming.

No teachers strive to be unprofessional. In fact, their screaming usually results from their desperate attempts to gain control in the best way they know how. But by yelling at students, or at anyone for that matter, you are publicly announcing that you have absolutely lost control—control of yourself and control of your classroom environment.

Now think about this: Here we are, teachers, serving as role models for our students, hoping to influence the people that they are and will become. One of the most important things that we can ever hope to teach our students is that, in any given situation, though we cannot control the actions of others, we can always remain in control of ourselves. Therefore, it should not be an option for a teacher to raise his or her voice and scream at a student—unless, of course, the student is about to run out in front of a bus!

Yes, teaching can be frustrating. Yes, students *will* be aggravating from time to time. They're children—it's their job! But our job, as teachers, is to guide them gently and teach them a love of learning and a respect for others.

So what can you do instead of yelling and screaming when a student does not comply with your wishes? You can do what the most effective teachers do, by being serious yet soft-spoken. You can attack the problem without attacking the person. The more *out* of control a student becomes, the more *in* control an effective teacher must be. Without fail, the most effective teachers all agree that **it is *never* appropriate or effective to yell or scream at a student.** Period. So how do they control themselves? They just do it. They have all made a conscious decision that no matter how aggravated they become, they will never lose their professionalism.

Lost within a Shout

You yelled at me and I yelled back—what else was there to do?

We yelled some more and our throats got sore, and the tension grew and grew

And finally, in exhaustion, we both ran out of steam

Left standing in embarrassment, no pride left to redeem

What point is there in thinking that to be "right" we must

Keep pushing on till all involved just lose respect and trust?

Maybe if we'd listened, we could have met half way

Let's talk next time and really hear what the other has to say

For if we both could do that, maybe we'd find out

That never has a point been made when lost within a shout!

Secret Two—Chapter Summary

Regarding classroom management, remember the following:

- ◆ Follow the blueprint we provided on page 22 under the heading "What an Effective Teacher's Classroom Looks Like."
- ◆ Remember that rules have consequences and procedures do not.
- ◆ Allow students to take ownership of the classroom rules.
- ◆ Remain consistent regarding the implementation of rules and procedures.
- ◆ Teach from bell to bell.
- ◆ Be proactive in your approach to discipline.
- ◆ Don't become the dreaded screamer.
- ◆ Be aware that the more out of control a student gets, the more in control you must become.

Secret Three

The Secret of Instruction

Secret 3.

Make It Real

I just don't see the point in why I need to know this junk
You say if I don't learn it, then surely I will flunk
But I need a better reason for learning all this stuff
It's boring and it's pointless, so learning it is rough
And every time I'm bored in school, I think of other things
Lost inside a daydream until the school bell rings
Which means I haven't learned it, which means my grades are bad
Which means that I'm in trouble and my mom and dad are mad
And then I get so far behind that it's just too late to pass
So next year here I am again—I'm right back in your class
I didn't get it last year; I don't get it today
Please, teacher, make it real for me so that I can move on in May!

Part 1.
How to Teach for Real Life

When asked the question "What is real-life teaching?" most teachers will respond that real-life teaching means relating the skills they teach to real life. They're correct—partially. But they've quite possibly missed the absolute key component in the definition of true real-life teaching. This is the component that the most effective teachers always include in their definition of real-life teaching. The very best teachers will define real-life teaching as follows:

Real-life teaching means relating the skills I teach to the real lives of my students!

We sincerely believe that all teachers teach their students in the best way they know how. And that leads us to assume that many teachers simply do not *know* what the best teachers know. If they did, they would do what the best teachers do! And thus, of course, the purpose of this book—to share the secrets of the very best teachers so that other willing teachers can join these ranks.

To illustrate the difference between teaching for real life and teaching for the real lives of our students, we ask that you follow us into two teachers' classrooms. The first teacher, Teacher A, is doing the best she can. She is not clear on the actual definition of real-life teaching. The second teacher, Teacher B, understands that to teach for real life means to teach every skill based on the importance of that particular skill to the real lives of her students.

Both are teaching their students about pronouns. First, let's look in on Teacher A.

Teacher A

Teacher A has the students take out their English books and open to page 24. After much balking and squawking, the students are finally ready to proceed. Teacher A announces that today they will be learning about pronouns. She reads the definition from the text: "A pronoun takes the place of a noun." She then points out the list of sample pronouns below the definition. Students are instructed to write the definition of a pronoun in their notebooks along with the list of sample pronouns. Next, Teacher A writes a sentence on the board that reads, "Bobby went to the store." She then shows the students that the noun *Bobby* may be replaced with the pronoun *He.* Several other sentences are written on the board, and students are asked to replace select nouns with appropriate pronouns. Following this activity, the students are instructed to complete Exercise A in the textbook. For Exercise A, they must underline the pronouns. It is interesting to note that not one student appears in any way excited or enthusiastic. Many students are talking, and Teacher A begs and pleads with some of the students to "Get busy."

One student asks, "Why do we have to know this?" Teacher A responds by saying, "You need to know this so that you can speak English correctly. Without proper English, you won't be able to get a decent job when you grow up." This, of course, does not appease the student, as he fails to see the relevance of pronouns in his life today!

When this exercise is completed, Teacher A goes over the correct answers with the class. This, of course, is followed by Exercise B, and, finally, the dreaded worksheet on pronouns. The test, not surprisingly, will be on Friday. The fact is that most of the students will probably pass the test. However, do any of the students know how their own lives would be drastically affected were pronouns to be removed from the language? Do they even know why pronouns exist? Yes, they can state that a pronoun takes the place of a noun, but do they know why? Not unless they've figured this out on their own, and most have not.

Now let's take a look at a very different kind of lesson, also on pronouns. This lesson occurs in the classroom of Teacher B.

Teacher B

Teacher B smiles enthusiastically and says, "I've written a list of words on the board, and we are going to try *not* to use any of these words." Note that he doesn't yet mention the textbook, the term *pronouns*, or anything else for that matter. Instead, he asks Paul to tell something about himself without using any of the words on the board. (The words on the board, of course, are pronouns.) Paul begins by saying, "I like to..." and Teacher B stops him immediately, saying, "You used the word 'I,' which is on the board." Paul thinks about that and can't seem to figure out how to say something about himself without using the word *I*. Teacher B then says, "Paul, I'll give you a little time to figure it out while Beth gives it a shot." Beth, of course, begins struggling also. The teacher then explains that the students must refer to themselves by name. He provides an example, and the students seem to understand. But they laugh, because calling themselves by their own names sounds awkward. Students are then instructed to write one sentence telling something about themselves without using any of the words on the board. The students then read their sentences aloud. They anxiously participate.

Next, the teacher puts a short paragraph on the overhead projector and says, "Let's find all of the words in the paragraph that are listed on the board and cross them out." The words they cross out must then be replaced with words that are not on the board. In other words, they have to replace the pronouns with the nouns that the pronouns are representing. However, the terms *pronouns* and *nouns* have not yet been used by the teacher. The paragraph, of course, sounds awkward once the pronouns have been replaced.

And now on to the next activity. (Please notice how brief each activity is. This keeps it interesting, and it keeps the lesson moving quickly.) For this activity, one student is to begin telling something about himself to the class in a conversational way. He is to attempt to *not* use any of the words (pronouns) on the board. If and when he does, the class shouts "Stop!" and another student gets a chance.

You see, it has already become obvious to the students that these words, whatever they are, are necessary to our language. Without them, it would be very awkward to speak or to write, or even to think, for that matter.

Finally, the teacher does tell the class that these words are called *pronouns* and that pronouns take the place of nouns. He has the students explain what just happened in the preceding activities and discussing how awkward it was not to use these pronouns.

"So why do you think we have pronouns in our language?" asks the teacher. Any student in this classroom has already figured out that pronouns don't just take the place of nouns for the sake of taking the place of nouns, but rather they make the language flow smoothly and sound less awkward. The fact is that all of our lives would be drastically affected were pronouns to be taken out of the language. We would have trouble completing a sentence, much less getting our points across to others.

Question: Do you see the difference that it makes once students know how a skill they are learning affects their lives? **The fact is that if something seems relevant to us, we become interested.** And once we are interested, we are more apt to learn whatever it is that is relevant!

Please understand that we are in no way opposed to the use of textbooks. Teacher B actually went on to use one of the exercises in the textbook *after* he had established the real-life relevance of pronouns.

To attempt to teach anything to anyone without first establishing a real-life connection is practically futile. And that is one of the keys to what sets the very best teachers apart from the rest—they teach everything to their students by relating all of it to the real lives of their students, *today!* We stress the word *today* because many teachers, like Teacher A, explain to their students that the skill will be important someday when they are grown. Children cannot relate to *someday*. Even high school seniors are capable of thinking only as far into the future as Friday night!

> So make your lessons exciting and inviting by relating what you teach to the students' lives today!

Part 2.
How to Ensure Active Student Involvement

Maybe the term *active student involvement* should be changed to *intentional student involvement*. Let us explain. In any given classroom, if students are present, there is active student involvement. However, in some classrooms, students are actively involved in daydreaming, actively involved in sleeping, actively involved in their discussions with one another regarding the latest hair-braiding technique, actively involved in practicing the latest hair-braiding technique (you get the picture). These types of active student involvement, we firmly believe, are never intentional on the parts of the teachers in whose classrooms they take place.

All teachers would like to see their students actively engaged in meaningful, purposeful learning. So why is it not commonplace in all classrooms? The reason is that not all teachers are doing what the most effective teachers are doing. That, of course, is our intention in writing this book—to share with all teachers what works, based on the successes of the very best teachers. And so, regarding active student involvement, **the very best teachers plan lessons and activities that involve their students in every part of every lesson.** Yes, the students do the doing, and that is intentional. Active student involvement is neither an accident nor a welcomed surprise.

So how do they do it? Here's how. The very best teachers plan specific questions they will ask their students; they actually anticipate student questions; they determine how their students, based on life experiences, will best be able to relate to and understand the new skills being taught; and they plan activities that will cause students to think, to reason, to analyze, to question, and, finally, to understand.

Note: Active (intentional) student involvement is not reserved for elementary classrooms! Learning is an active process, regardless of age. But, typically, the higher the grade level, the less active student involvement we tend to see in the classroom. This is a mistake, as it is not true that to prepare students for college or for real life we need to give copious amounts of notes and have them read ridiculously long amounts of text on their own. And, of course, it is not to say that all secondary teachers' classrooms lack active, intentional student involvement. It is to say, however, that in far too many classrooms, from elementary through secondary, there is a definite lack of such engagement. Again, it's one of the factors that separate the very best teachers from the less effective ones.

Walk into an effective teacher's classroom and you will rarely see students seated, silently doing busy work. Instead, you will both sense and see excitement, questioning, problem solving, and so forth. Conversely, in the classrooms of less effective teachers, the air seems heavy and the classroom seems lifeless. And oftentimes, these teachers blame the lack of activity on the students or the material: "These students can't handle activity. They argue, they talk, and things get totally out of hand," or "The subject matter that I teach does not lend itself to activity."

Well, given that our beliefs become our realities, it stands to reason that these teachers' classrooms are sorely lacking in active student involvement.

Oh, we should probably add another explanation for lack of activity: "That's the way I learned, and I survived it!" Consider this: In days long past, anesthetic consisted of a bullet and a bottle of whiskey! That, of course, was not wrong or bad in those days, as there was not yet a better way. And, though the pain was excruciating, people actually did survive! Today, of course, if you went into the operating room and were handed a bullet and a bottle of whiskey, you would run out into the street with no consideration being given to your less than appropriate attire. That, of course, is because you know that there is a better way! And so it is in teaching. We know a better way!

When they threw out the bullet and the bottle of whiskey

There were those who said it was risky

But thank goodness some were willing to try

A better way—no one will deny

And so, fellow teachers, give change a chance

Let your students learn; let them dance!

Part 3.
How to Ensure Success for All Students

The very best teachers all agree that if you want a student to succeed, then you have to first make him successful. At first glance, this may seem contradictory, but in actuality, it's not. It goes along with the old adage "Success breeds success." **The most effective teachers refuse to believe that there is any such thing as a student not capable of succeeding and achieving.** They never give up on *any* student. In fact, the students who appear to be the least successful always get the most attention and the most patience from the most effective teachers! Conversely, in the classrooms of less effective teachers, these are the same students who are often ignored. The reason for this, we believe, is simply that these teachers do not know how to make these students successful.

So how do you make any student successful? You teach him at his or her level. Are we opening that can of worms again? No, we are simply stating a fact. And the fact is that the only level at which anyone can learn is his or her own level. We have always been baffled by educated people who argue whether we should teach students "at grade level" or "at their level." Again, you can only learn at one person's level—and that is your own!

Consider learning a language that is foreign to you. You are placed in a classroom of students who are advanced learners, quite fluent in the language. You, on the other hand, are an absolute novice. Thus, you will eventually realize that no matter how hard you try, you will not be successful in learning and speaking the language, because you have missed its very foundation. You will soon do one of two things: Either you will zone out, or you will become a behavior problem. After all, what else is there to do when you just don't understand anything that is being said or done in the classroom? Imagine, however, that the teacher realized your lack of skill in speaking this language and thus altered your activities to ensure success. By teaching you the basics of the language, the teacher would ensure some immediate success for you. And because success is gratifying, you would want to work even harder to achieve even more success. That, our fellow educators, is just plain good teaching.

Let's be clear on the fact that, as teachers, we understand that it is not easy to meet the needs of so many students at so many levels at one time. That, of course, is why effective teaching is truly an art. It is never easy, but always rewarding.

The bottom line is that there simply is no other way to teach students than at their own levels. As teachers, it is our responsibility and our purpose to do whatever it takes to ensure success for *each* of our students, not *most* of them. So…

> Teach a student at his level, and in his successes you both will revel. And that success will lead to another—a better way, there is no other!

Part 4.
How to Teach Enthusiastically

Have you ever gone to hear a motivational speaker and been sorely disappointed and, to top it off, bored out of your mind? You were, by the way, within your rights to be sorely disappointed, as you were expecting to be motivated. Well, let's carry that idea into a school as we take a look at two teachers teaching the very same subject matter. First, let's go into "Ms. Teaching Is a Chore's" (Ms. Tic's) classroom.

Ms. Tic

The students enter the room with Ms. Tic standing at the door with her "I dare you to even think about misbehaving" look. Of course, being students, they take the dare and immediately begin to misbehave. Ms. Tic doles out several empty threats and warnings, and finally the students settle down. Ms. Tic then tells the students to open their social studies books to page 97. After several more threats and warnings, Ms. Tic says, with the inflection of a robot, "Today we'll be talking about the Brooklyn Bridge. Now write 'The Brooklyn Bridge' in your notebooks." The students reluctantly do so, and Ms. Tic begins to read from the text. Again, with no inflection, she tells the students to copy the first sentence into their notebooks as she reads it aloud—it goes something along the lines of the following (we'll try to make it sound like her).

"The Brooklyn Bridge, The Brooklyn Bridge, don't forget to capitalize that, which spans the river between, spans the river between, spans the river between Manhattan, Manhattan, Manhattan (and a student asks how to spell Manhattan as Ms. Tic tells him to look at his book and continues without skipping a beat) and Brooklyn was dedicated, was dedicated, was ded… (and a student interrupts and says that Ms. Tic is going too fast, and Ms. Tic scowls and continues) in 1883. It has a span, it has a span, it has a span of 1600 feet…."

Okay, you get the picture—that is, if you haven't fallen asleep. The class finally takes the notes (the same ones that are already in the textbook, so we aren't sure why they have to copy what's already accessible to them), and Ms. Tic spits out a few facts about a suspension bridge. The students are simply not listening. Most are talking, sleeping, meditating, or whatever else it is that students do when they are not interested. Ms. Tic consistently stops to scold them about not paying attention. After she has finished with the initial note-taking activity, she tells them to finish reading the chapter. And you know the rest of the story.

Question: Did you sense even a hint of enthusiasm on the part of the Ms. Tic? Where did she go wrong?

Now let's look in on Ms. Enthusiastic's classroom.

Ms. Enthusiastic

Ms. Enthusiastic anxiously (or so she appears) awaits the arrival of her students, as she does every day, with a big smile and welcoming demeanor. The students walk in and sit down, and there's Ms. Enthusiastic, smiling as always. She begins by saying, "I can't wait to share this story with you. It's about the Brooklyn Bridge and the people who built it, and it's fascinating. Don't even bother to take out your books right now. I just want for you to sit back and enjoy this amazing true story." She goes on to tell them about John Roebling, the man who conceived the idea of building the bridge, and then about how Roebling was killed in an onsite accident while the bridge was being built. The students are all ears, and the rest of the story is truly fascinating. When the story is finished, the teacher begins, enthusiastically, to question the students about what was so innovative about the idea of a suspension bridge. The discussion leads to more questions, and then Ms. Enthusiastic says, "I think I know where we can find those answers. Let's get into our cooperative groups. The students do so with a sense of order, and it is obvious that there are clearly established procedures in place in this classroom. Ms. Enthusiastic thanks them for getting into their groups so quickly, and she then tells them to open their books to page 97. Because she knows the secret of effective planning, she has already devised separate assignments for each group. In short, they will all be reading different sections of the chapter—short sections, of course—for a very specific purpose. Once they have read their assigned sections within their groups, they answer some very specific questions and then report their findings to the rest of the class. Ms. Enthusiastic enthusiastically walks around the room, appearing to be engrossed in each group's discussion. The lesson progresses with more activities, each designed to involve the students in thinking, wondering, questioning, and learning about something truly fascinating.

Okay, so isn't it obvious what went right in the classroom of Ms. Enthusiastic? The fact is that she has probably taught this lesson many times over the years, but each group of students is a new group, so she teaches as if it is the most exciting thing she's ever taught. By the way, she does this with every lesson she teaches every day!

As an aside, Ms. Tic is stopping at the drugstore this afternoon to refill her ulcer medication. Ms. Enthusiastic is meeting friends for happy hour!

The bottom line is that students need to think that everything you teach is something you love to teach. But what if you just don't feel enthusiastic about what you're teaching? Then do what the most effective teachers do and *fake it!* You see, as teachers, we are all human, and none of us are happy all of the time. We all have bad days. But the fact remains that students learn and behave best in the classrooms of enthusiastic teachers.

> So teach enthusiastically, and student learning will improve drastically!

Part 5.
How to Align Teaching and Testing

One of the best-kept secrets of the most effective teachers is that they test only what they teach. We'll repeat that—**they test only what they teach,** and, to add to that recipe for success, **they actually test what they have taught in the same way that they have taught it!** This may seem oversimplified, but the fact remains that not all teachers actually test the same things that they teach in the same way that they have taught them.

First, let's discuss *testing what we teach*. Imagine that you are a student in a classroom, and on Monday, you begin a new reading story. Throughout the course of the week, you define the vocabulary words assigned by the teacher, you read the story silently, your class suffers through the typical round-robin reading (in which the entire story is read orally), you answer the story questions, you discuss the story, and so on. Question: What has been taught? What new reading strategies have you learned? And let's, for the sake of argument, say that you actually have been taught the skill of *identifying the main idea* as you read. Your test, of course, is on Friday. And on Friday's test, you match the vocabulary words to their definitions and you answer the typical questions such as: Who was the author of the story? Where did the story take place? Who was the main character? What problem did the main character face? How was the problem resolved?

Now, because you studied the notes and heard the answers to these questions all week, you memorized the answers and did a darned good job of it—good enough to make an A on the reading test. But even if you are a poor reader, is it not true that you could have aced that test by studying extra hard? In other words, that was not really a reading test. It was a *remembering* test. And where on the test did you *identify the main idea*? Wouldn't you have to read unfamiliar text to demonstrate your knowledge of that skill or any other?

The story in the textbook was provided, initially, to help you learn and practice one or more new reading skills, but to use the same story on the test is not aligning teaching and testing. This, of course, is only one example, but you get the idea. The fact remains that many teachers "test" reading this way, but they're not actually testing reading!

Now let's move on to **testing the way we teach**. A teacher recently gave her students a list of vocabulary words to memorize. The students were to find the definitions in the dictionary and copy the definitions in their notes. The class, as a group, went over the definitions with the teacher. And then on the test, the directions were to use each of the words in a sentence. Many students, of course, did not do well on the test. Is it any wonder? You see, not once had the words actually been *used* in class. The definitions were simply memorized, and the teacher assumed that the students, once they had the definitions *memorized*, would be able to transfer their knowledge to actually using the words. Huge mistake!

If you want your students to do something on a test, then teach them how to do it, practice doing it with them, have them practice on their own while you monitor, and then test them in the same way that they have been practicing whatever it is that you have taught in the *same* way that you have taught it. That, in a nutshell, is what the very best teachers do differently from everyone else!

Think of it this way: If you took swimming lessons—with the objective, of course, being that you would learn to swim—and were seated with your classmates in rows beside the pool, and you defined all the swimming vocabulary words and then listened to the lecture on swimming, and then read the chapter on swimming, and then answered the questions at the end of the chapter on swimming, and then watched your teacher model swimming, and then watched the video on swimming, and then studied all the notes and memorized them and, for your test, were asked to actually swim, could you do it? Notice that even though the teacher talked about swimming all week and taught you the vocabulary, the names of the different strokes, and so forth, and actually modeled swimming for you, the way that you were tested was nothing like what you had been taught. Learning the rules and terminology of swimming is *not* the same as actually swimming. And that's why students drown every day in some teachers' classrooms. So remember:

> Align what you teach with what you test, and you'll get from students their very best!

Part 6.
How to Pace Your Lessons Appropriately

Part of the secret of effective instruction is making sure that your lessons move along at a quick yet appropriate pace. A new teacher was told by her principal that she needed to pick up her pace while teaching. The next time the principal observed, the teacher spoke so quickly that neither the students nor the principal could understand what she was saying. Thank goodness, the principal realized what had happened and then clarified what he meant by picking up the pace. Of course, it does not mean that you should talk really fast. It means that your lesson's activities should move along so that students remain involved and actively engaged and do not zone out. When a lesson is paced appropriately, things move quickly, students are active, and there is never a dull moment or an empty moment with nothing to do. Everything simply flows along smoothly, and you can feel it flowing.

Even the best teachers will tell you, however, that this skill takes some practice, but once you get the feel for a well-paced lesson, you soon become proficient.

The following are a few **tips to let you know if your lesson is appropriately paced:**

- The students appear interested.
- Your voice sounds enthusiastic.
- You actually feel enthusiastic while teaching.
- You move quickly from one activity to the next, but never so quickly that you leave the students in the dust.
- If students do not understand, you immediately do some reteaching.
- Your transitions from one activity to the next move quickly and in an orderly way.
- The time seems to fly by, and the bell has rung before you know it.
- Students seem to understand what you are teaching!

Conversely, here are some **warning signs that your lesson is moving too slowly:**

- You observe dull, blank stares of boredom from students.
- Even *you* actually feel bored.
- The lesson feels like it's dragging along.

- Students lack enthusiasm during the activities
- The air in the room feels heavy.
- Students are, or at least appear to be, sleeping.
- Your head jerks and you are suddenly awakened, embarrassed. The good news is that no one notices. Remember, they're also sleeping!

Seriously, practice pacing the lesson to get the feel of it. Videotape yourself if necessary. But the absolute best way to judge whether your lesson is paced appropriately is by simply observing the behaviors of your students.

Bottom line?

They'll let you know if you go too slow, as the looks on their faces will be empty places. If you go too fast, they'll show their frustration, but get it just right and you'll see concentration. Their faces tell all, so look and you'll know if your lesson is paced appropriately so!

Part 7.
How to Teach Anything to Anyone

The most effective teachers know that if you're going to teach anything to anyone, you must **establish a relationship** between the new skill and the student's real life, **teach and model** the new skill, **practice** the new skill with the student, allow the student to **try the new skill** on his or her own, and **review**, over and over, providing as much guidance and practice as necessary. That's it! This is nothing new. This is not rocket science. Its effectiveness has been proven time and again. Yet many teachers do not follow these simple steps in teaching. And it is truly one of the determining factors in separating the most effective teachers from the less effective ones.

So here it is, plainly and simply:

The first step has been called the *introduction,* the *anticipatory set,* the *task focus,* and so on. We really don't care what you call it, as long as you do it. This is where you **secure the students' attention and relate the skill to their real lives** so that they will actually want to learn what you will be teaching. Much interaction and discussion should take place here, as opposed to the teacher simply reading the objective to the students and telling them why they need this skill.

Next, you will actually **teach the new skill.** And please do not ever forget to model the skill for the students. Teaching involves much more than just telling.

After you have taught the new skill, **practice it with the students.** Most of us know this as *guided practice,* in which the teacher and students practice together. That's right. The teacher practices with the students, monitoring constantly for understanding. During this part of the lesson, you'll get a really good sense of who understands and who is still struggling. If everyone seems to be struggling, you will immediately know to do some reteaching. But if it appears that most, if not all, of the students understand, you move on to the next logical step, which is to **let them try the new skill on their own.** At this point, you'll either be monitoring while they practice independently or you'll be working on more guided practice with the few who are not yet ready for independent practice.

And, of course, don't ever forget to **review what has been learned.** How do you go about this? We always suggest that you plan some type of activity in which the students tell or show what they have learned, as opposed to the teacher's telling or showing them what they have learned.

And that's it! That's how to teach anything to anyone. It can be applied to teaching someone to drive, to cook, to ski, to swim, to tie shoelaces, to write a paragraph, to analyze patterns, to diagram sentences, to follow the steps of the scientific method, or anything else.

Again, this is not rocket science. Imagine that your young child is going off to summer camp. You know that he will be taught how to use matches, yet you definitely want to teach him that lesson *before* someone else teaches him. So, wouldn't it make sense that you would sit with your child and (1) tell him what he'll be learning and why he'll be learning it, relating, of course, to the fact that he will be learning to use matches at camp soon, so you're teaching him in advance; (2) actually teach him to use matches, not just by telling but by modeling the skill and by discussing the proper uses of matches, the improper uses of matches, and so on. You would (3) guide him and practice with him as you hold his hand at first. Once he becomes successful enough with your guidance, you would (4) have him try the new skill on his own as you monitor, and, finally, (5) for closure, review and discuss all you have learned, allowing him to demonstrate, once again, what he now knows. There it is—just plain good teaching! There is no step that can be justifiably skipped.

It should look no different in the classroom, yet it often does. Teachers leave one or two steps out, or they send the students off to try a new skill on their own without proper guided practice, or they "tell" how something should be done without actually modeling it for the students. Again, it's one of the major differences between effective and less effective teachers. The most effective teachers follow all of the steps all of the time.

> Introduce the new skill and get my attention
> As this will increase my chance of retention
> Then tell me about it and show me as well
> By showing me how, my fears you will quell
> Then guide me along as I try the new skill
> Helping me reach the top of that hill
> And then let me try independently
> But don't be so far away that you can't see
> And once I've got it, you've opened the door
> So now let's review it over and more.

Secret Three—Chapter Summary

Regarding effective instruction, remember the following:

- Relate everything you teach to the real lives of your students.
- Plan lessons and activities that will actively involve your students.
- Make all students successful by teaching them at their level and then moving them forward.
- Be enthusiastic in your teaching, and when you don't feel enthusiastic, fake it!
- Test only what you teach.
- Test in the same way that you have taught.
- Pace your lessons such that activities move quickly, students remain active, and there is never any downtime when students have nothing to do.
- Follow the basic steps we've outlined for teaching anything to anyone!

Secret Four

The Secret of Attitude

We Get to Choose

One saw a glass half empty
The other, a glass half full
What? It was the same glass?
What stunt were they trying to pull?
No stunt was pulled at all, you see
Our attitudes shape our vision
We all get to choose for ourselves
Whether life's an adventure or a collision!

Part 1.
How to Be in Control of Your Attitude: It's Up to You!

The very best teachers agree that attitude is everything! **One of the main things that separate the not-so-good from the good from the great teachers is simply attitude.**

We have all been treated in ways that we wish we had not. We may have relatives, coworkers, supervisors, or neighbors who are unpleasant to be around. Any time we are near them, we feel on guard and try to protect ourselves from their next cutting remark. It seems that their main goal in life is to make everyone else as unhappy as they are. Sadly, some of these people become teachers, and each of us has known at least one or two. What's really frightening is that negative people don't know they're negative!

Ms. Idkin (**I Don't Know I'm Negative**) was recently observed by her principal. Throughout the lesson, it seemed that you couldn't see the teaching through the negative comments. Reprimands such as "Stop it"; "Don't even think about it"; "Be quiet"; "If you do it again…"; "I said to pay attention"; "You know that answer. We studied that last week"; "How many times do I have to tell you?" spilled angrily from Ms. Idkin. Following the lesson, the principal sat with Ms. Idkin and told her he would like for her to try to be a little more positive with the students. Ms. Idkin barked, "I was positive! I said 'good'!" Ms. Idkin was actually correct in that she had uttered the word *good* to one student who had a correct answer. But in her mind, saying the word *good* made her positive. Her perceptions illustrate that negative people do not see themselves as negative, and that can be dangerous!

So what do you do when you have a coworker who is negative—or when that person teaches right next door to you? We posed this question to an effective teacher, and she said, "I simply model, model, model." When asked what she meant by this, she replied, "Well, I have no control over her attitude, only mine. So I just stay positive and hope that maybe a little of it may one day rub off on her. If it doesn't, I haven't lost a thing, and I still get to keep my sanity!"

In an interview, a less than effective, more than slightly negative teacher complained by saying, "Things are bad in our schools today because everything in the world is negative. The news on television is negative, the newspaper headlines are negative, and these students' parents are negative also.

So it's hard to stay positive when you're bombarded with so many negatives in society."

Regrettably, what this teacher failed to realize was that her role as a teacher is not to reflect current society—at least not the negative parts of it. Her role, as is that of every teacher, is to cultivate and help shape the future of society! Let's say, for the sake of argument, that this teacher is in some ways correct. Let's say that there is too much negative media coverage, that there are some negative parents out there, and that some aspects of society are just downright negative. Okay, then this teacher now has a choice. She can either give in and perpetuate those negative attitudes in her students, or she can choose to teach them a better way! The best teachers always choose a better way. That's what teaching is all about—breaking bad habits, forging new paths, opening doors, and leading students to make different and better choices and to have better attitudes.

We've all taught students who were lacking in manners and in positive attitudes. It's a fact that some students simply do not know how to do things we often take for granted, such as apologizing when they've done something wrong, saying "excuse me" if they bump into someone else, or raising their hands instead of just blurting out their answers. *We're* the adults. We're supposed to show them *how*.

We've also met the teachers who blame the parents for not teaching their children any manners. The bottom line is that there are students in classrooms every day who lack basic manners and social graces. So we have a choice. As their teachers, as the cultivators of a future society, we can choose to continue to whine and complain about the fact that the students are lacking in manners, or we can remain in control of our attitudes by simply teaching and modeling the appropriate behaviors. The very best teachers, of course, always do the latter.

As teachers, we, and *only* we, get to choose our attitudes every day. Regardless of how negative some coworkers are, how negative the news may be on a given day, how negative some students may be, we cannot let the actions of others shape our attitudes.

> We are the teachers. We are the leaders. We are the role models. Every day, our attitudes help to shape the types of teachers, leaders, and role models we become.

Part 2.
How to Handle Yourself in the Teachers' Lounge

There is not a college teacher-preparation program anywhere that offers a course called "Griping, Groaning, and Gossiping in the Teachers' Lounge." Yet, every now and then, hopefully not too often, we come across a new teacher who has mastered and refined those skills by the middle of October! How is this possible, and where did the new teacher learn these skills? Not surprisingly, there is an unofficial, nonaccredited course in some schools that takes place every day in the teachers' lounge.

Consider the meaning of the term *teachers' lounge.* Doesn't it suggest a place for teachers to be able to put their feet up and relax? Though we do not know who coined the term, we are quite positive that that is what the inventor of the first teachers' lounge intended it to be—a place for teachers to relax and unwind. Yet, in some schools, the lounge has become a place where some teachers like to gripe, groan, and gossip.

We wholeheartedly believe that teachers are inherently good people. We also believe that the gossips—and they're out there—have never stopped to analyze what they're doing, much less to consider the fact that **gossip basically serves one purpose—it** *harms!* Our purpose, as teachers, is not to harm anyone or hurt anyone's feelings. We're the ones who are supposed to lift others, not kick them. Another fact that the gripers, groaners, and gossips fail to realize is that no one respects them. They don't even respect one another. Remember, the old rule says that if someone will gossip *with* you, he or she will also gossip *about* you!

A seminar was held for teachers who were preparing to become principals. There was a lengthy discussion as to whether teachers should even consider applying for a principal's position in the same school where they were currently teaching, should such a position become available. Several teachers, along with the administrators conducting the seminar, described instances in which teachers had become principals in the same schools where they had taught. In some cases, it worked. In other cases, it was a *bad* move. So these situations were further analyzed, and something interesting was uncovered. The only times it was counterproductive for a teacher to become a principal in his or her own school was when the teacher was a well-known griper, groaner, and gossip. In these cases, the faculty members had no respect for this person, so they could definitely not take this person seriously as the new principal.

The fact is that being around negative people is *never* likely to have a positive impact on you. Consider the following: Four teachers are having a positive and friendly conversation over lunch, and a fifth teacher, Ms. Crabapple, joins then. Ms. Crabapple immediately does what Ms. Crabapple always does—whines and complains about her students, the principal, the parents, her family, and life in general. Immediately, the entire mood of the conversation and of the people engaged in the conversation changes. Thank goodness the other four teachers are effective teachers and are able to tactfully put an end to the conversation and leave. It's not surprising, by the way, that the teachers engaged in the prior positive conversation were all effective teachers. It's a fact that water seeks its own level. Positive, effective teachers associate themselves with other positive teachers. Negative teachers, likewise, associate with other negative teachers. There's comfort in shared misery—at least in their minds. What's dangerous is that these negative teachers seem to actively seek new recruits.

So how do the most effective teachers handle the lounge? Do they just stay away? We went to them and asked just that. Here's what they had to say:

- ◆ "I've taught in several schools over my 30-plus years in the classroom, and in every one of those schools, there were a few negative teachers. Early on in my career, I used to avoid the teachers' lounge completely. But then I realized that I could go in there, have a cup of coffee, and simply not participate in any negative conversations. In fact, a few of us soon realized that if enough positive teachers bombarded the lounge with positive conversations, the negative tone would soon change. And it worked. That's not to say that a few negative teachers don't visit the teachers' lounge anymore, but the rest of us make it really difficult for them to feel comfortable in their griping. It's kind of fun, actually!"

- ◆ "Yes, there will always be a few negative teachers, I suppose, on any faculty, but I just make sure I don't hang around those people. I don't go to the lounge very often, but when I do, I keep my conversations upbeat and positive. I can't control their moods or actions, but I can surely control mine."

- ◆ "My principal put a sign on the lounge door that says, 'No Whining.' We literally have a rule stating that no teacher can complain about *anything* in the teachers' lounge. Needless to say, a few teachers have since boycotted the lounge. But those were the people the rule was made for anyway! So our lounge is really a pleasant place these days."

◆ "Gossip doesn't only happen in the lounge. It happens any time two or more negative people get together anywhere in the school. Whenever coworkers approach me and try to gossip or complain, I always pretend that I have to go to the bathroom and tell them I'll talk to them later! In the meantime, I guess they tell someone else, because they never come back to me later."

Having read what these teachers have to say, do you see a commonality? Did you notice that all of them simply refuse to participate in the negative chatter? We can all admit that sometimes it would be easy just to blow off some steam and spurt out some negative comments, but we must also admit that it simply would not be professional. And as we are all supposed to be professionals, being unprofessional is simply not an option!

> Always do what a professional does and stay away from the negative buzz!

Part 3.
How to Improve the Attitudes of Your Students

In a perfect world, all students would come to us eager to learn, enthusiastic about anything we have to teach, and positive in their attitudes about life and learning. But, as any teacher knows, that's not reality. Some students come to us with less-than-appropriate attitudes, and they often pose a threat to the positive climate of our classrooms. This, of course, is where effective teachers work their magic.

Come along with us as we follow Michael (a student who wears a very large chip on his shoulder) into two of his classes. You decide which teacher is more effective in dealing with Michael.

Teacher A

Michael walks into the classroom in a bad mood. The teacher immediately sees that he is upset and stops him at the door. "Michael, it seems that you're really upset about something. Is there anything I can do to help?" Michael proceeds to tell the teacher that he's tired of people picking on him at recess. The teacher says, "I can understand how that would be very upsetting. If you'd like, we'll talk some more about this after everyone has started on their work, and I promise I'll do my best to help you resolve this problem. In the meantime, I'd really appreciate your sitting quietly in your desk until we get a chance to talk. Thanks, Michael." Michael appears instantly calmer, and he goes to his desk quietly. He knows that someone cares and is even willing to help him with his problem.

Teacher B

Michael walks into the classroom in a bad mood. The teacher immediately sees that he is upset and barks, "Don't you dare bring whatever happened at recess into this room!" Michael barks back by saying, "I'm tired of everyone picking on me at recess!" The teacher says, "Well if you're acting with them the way you're acting now, I don't blame them for picking on you! Now sit down and be quiet. I don't want to hear another word about it." Michael storms over to his desk and slams his books on the floor. The teacher then says, "Now pick those books up right now, young man. You will *not* act this way in *my* classroom!" Michael then replies with words we will not repeat and is sent to the office.

Okay, we will not insult your intelligence by telling you which was the more appropriate way to handle Michael. We just wanted to make the point that the teacher's attitude and approach can either ignite a volatile situation or extinguish it.

Remember, we're role models. We're supposed to model appropriate ways to handle situations, not add fuel to the flames! **Our attitudes definitely spill over onto our students.** In the classrooms of calm, composed teachers, students tend to be more calm and composed. That is not to say that the Michaels of this world are always calm and composed. (Heck, we would not like being picked on very much, either. It's an awful feeling.) But the fact remains that **negative attitudes are never tempered by negative responses.**

Students watch us constantly. They take their cues from us. They notice *everything* we do. Isn't it true that your students notice when you get a haircut, when you change colognes or perfumes, and when you wear a new outfit? They really do take notice of us, and they tend to emulate our language, our mannerisms, and the ways we deal with various situations. If, for one second, you doubt that your students notice everything about you, then we offer a challenge to you. We challenge you to walk into your classroom and ask your students, "Would anyone care to imitate me?" They'll not only do it, but they'll do it well! They can walk like you, they can talk like you, and more. Try it. We dare you!

Because students do notice everything about us, we must take special care to ensure that they're noticing positive, appropriate ways to handle any situation. Does this mean that they will always emulate those positive and appropriate ways of handling their own situations? Of course not. Remember, *they* are the students, and *we* are the teachers.

> The more out of control a student is, the more in control we, as teachers, have to be in dealing with that student. Is it easy? No. Is it effective? Yes!

Part 4.
How to Portray an Attitude of Responsibility

When several students are receiving failing grades in a particular teacher's classroom, is it the fault of the students or the teacher? That depends on whom you ask! Effective teachers will *always* take responsibility when students are not succeeding in their classrooms. This is not to say that the students are totally blameless, but, regardless, effective teachers will always look to themselves first and ask, "What can I do differently?"

Consider another scenario: If patients are dying on one particular surgeon's operating table, is it the fault of the patients or the surgeon? Again, effective surgeons will always ask themselves, "What can I do differently?" We would never accept the following argument from a surgeon: "Look, they were unhealthy when they came to me. If they had taken better care of themselves, they wouldn't have gotten sick in the first place. So it's not my fault they didn't make it through the surgery!"

Ineffective teachers are often heard saying, "The students don't study like they're supposed to, and that's why they're failing. It's not my fault they're not passing my class." In contrast, effective teachers, like effective surgeons (thank goodness!) possess an attitude of responsibility. They actually take it personally if their students are not doing well under their care. And they should!

When we became teachers, we each signed a contract and agreed to be responsible for the success of our students. But legal documents aside, **isn't it true that we became teachers to help the students who need us the most?** The ones who, without our help and guidance, might not make it to the next grade or even through the next week?

Let's compare two typical scenarios in the classrooms of effective teachers (those who portray an attitude of responsibility) with the same scenarios in the classrooms of less effective teachers (those who choose an attitude of "It's not my fault!").

Scenario 1: Student Sleeping in Class

Ineffective teachers will usually do one of two things: (1) they will let sleeping dogs lie, thankful that the student is at least not causing any problems while he's sleeping, or (2) they will reprimand the student for sleeping in class. Neither of these approaches, by the way, does anything to solve the problem.

Effective teachers will always speak to the student and find out what's causing him to fall asleep. Is it that the student is not getting a good night's sleep? Is it that the student is not feeling well? Or is he simply bored out of his mind? Determining what's causing the problem always helps the effective teacher to determine the best course of action for solving the problem.

Scenario 2: Grading Papers

Ineffective teachers use a technique called "trade and grade." They have their students trade papers and then grade one another's papers while the teacher calls out the correct answers. Some teachers even have the students call out the names and grades—for everyone to hear—from the papers they have graded, while the teacher quickly and efficiently records the grades in the grade book.

You may ask yourself, "Why would any teacher do this? Can't this be humiliating for the students who do not make good grades? And isn't it true that even students who make A's don't always want it broadcast to everyone?" The most likely answer to the first question is that teachers do this for their own convenience. It's quick, and it saves them the trouble of having to grade papers on their own time. Sad, but true. And yes, this technique can humiliate *any* student, regardless of what grade he or she earned.

When asked why she used this particular technique of grading papers, an ineffective teacher responded, "Students like immediate feedback, and this way they know how they scored on their tests immediately." When further questioned about the possibility of humiliating her students by using this method, she said, "Hey, if they're humiliated, it's their own fault. They should have studied harder."

Effective teachers use a technique we'll call "I grade my students' papers, just like a teacher is supposed to do!" We won't elaborate, because there's no need to. Effective teachers grade their students' papers, period.

> The fact is that the very best teachers accept responsibility for the success and performance of every student they teach.

Whether My Students Pass or Fail

He did not pass my test
Because he did not study
And so I took my red pen
And made his paper bloody
And then I started thinking
About what I was doing
What in the world was I trying to prove?
What point was I pursuing?
If studying determined his grade
What had I really taught?
If studying was the only way to pass
In class, no learning was wrought
Yes, studying is important,
But teaching should mean more
If I'm really teaching every day,
It should affect his score
Studying might make the difference
Between an A or a B
But whether my students pass or fail
Really depends on me!

Part 5.
How to Defuse Negative Coworkers

Though we have discussed the issue of dealing with negative coworkers in several places in the book, we thought it was worth adding this section to share with you some secrets that effective teachers use in defusing their negative counterparts. Here are a few of their tricks for defusing typical scenarios involving negative coworkers:

- If a coworker approaches you and begins to speak negatively about a student, try this: Simply say, "I love that kid. I know he's not always easy to deal with, but thank goodness he has us to help him learn better ways of dealing with life," and walk away.
- If a coworker approaches you and begins to gripe about something going on in the school, try this: Say, "I can appreciate your concerns. Why don't you talk to the principal and share those concerns? I'm sure he'd be happy to meet with you, and maybe the two of you can come up with a solution. It can't hurt to try!" and walk away.
- If a coworker tries to gossip with you about a student, teacher, parent, principal, or someone else, try this: Pretend that you are in a rush and will have to talk to him or her later, and walk away.
- If a coworker is reprimanding a student (in an unprofessional manner) in your presence, try this: Unless the student is in imminent bodily danger, walk away.
- If a coworker gripes constantly and you are simply at the end of your rope, try this: Say, "You seem really down today. You don't look well, either. Maybe you just need some rest when you get home," and walk away.
- If a coworker tries to engage you in a power struggle, try this: Walk away!

Notice that all suggestions end with "Walk away." Do your best at attempting to defuse these people, and then walk away. But whatever you do, don't participate in their negative conversations. And on days when you are feeling down or upset, don't go near them. You'll be much more tempted to give in on those days.

Finally, don't let them affect you. Yes, it is upsetting to be around negative people, so don't hang around them. Yes, it is disheartening to think that students are often the victims of negative teachers, but you can't control and are not responsible for the actions of these teachers, unless you are the principal!

> Interesting Fact: Walking away from negative people not only protects you from becoming one of them, it also burns calories!

Part 6.
How to Work Cooperatively with Parents

Dealing with parents, for some teachers, can be a frightening experience. We have learned that some teachers avoid any contact with parents if at all possible, because they are afraid of confrontations. This is a mistake. But why is it that the best teachers seem to just have a way of dealing with and working with parents so successfully? And why is it that others are so afraid of any contact with parents at all? Here's a fact: **Almost all parents do the very best they can, and they care deeply about their children.** You may or may not agree with how they raise their children, but they are doing the best they can. Regrettably, for some parents, the only times they hear from their children's teachers are when their children have done something wrong. So, these parents tend to be defensive. Some refuse to even answer their phones when someone from the school calls. They don't attend parent meetings and they don't show up for open house because they simply don't want to hear one more negative thing about their children. So what can we do to get parents more involved and to make sure that their experiences with their children's schools become more positive? We can do what the most effective teachers do.

The very best teachers keep in constant contact with the parents of their students. And they do this in a positive way. Here's a secret that one teacher shared with us:

"On the very first day of school each year, I give each of my students a note to bring to their parents. The note is a blanket note that I type and copy. It simply says, 'Dear [Name of parent], I am happy to be teaching your child, [Name of student], this year. Thank you for allowing your child to be in my class. Feel free to contact me at any time.'

"Then, every day, I make sure to write one note, per class, to a parent. Again, it's a little generic note that I have pre-typed and copied, ready to go. It simply says: 'Dear [Name of parent], I'm so proud of your child today because [Fill in reason].'

"I simply pick one student per class a day (sometimes two, as it only takes about 30 seconds to complete), and I write about something that this particular student did well that day. These are the kinds of notes that not only get delivered to parents but also get posted on the refrigerator! This ensures that every parent receives at least one positive note a month from me regarding his or her child's academic and/or behavioral successes. The parents think I'm the greatest teacher in the world, and they've never even seen me teach! Then, when I occasionally have to contact a parent regarding something negative about his or her child, the parent is unbelievably cooperative."

Some parents admit to this teacher that she is the first teacher to have ever told them anything positive about their children. This, of course, is a little thing that makes a big difference.

Another effective teacher said, "I always try to remember that the parents and I have the very same goal—the success of their child. Whenever I have to make a phone call to or meet with a parent regarding something negative his child has done, I always begin the conversation by saying, 'I know what a concerned parent you are, and I knew you would want to know what's going on. I think that if we work together, we can solve this problem.' This always seems to give me an advantage, as I've just complimented the parent on his concern for his child and told him I would like to work *with* him."

When asked how to deal with a confrontational parent—you know, the one who comes to school and wants to attack you in some way—a very effective teacher shared the following:

"I know that when a parent is angry with me, the last thing I want to do is engage in a power struggle by trying to defend myself. Instead, I calmly let the parent say what he has to say, and then I say, 'I can tell you're really upset, which tells me you're a concerned parent. I admire that. And I just want you to know that even if you and I don't agree today, I respect you for caring so much and feeling so passionate about your child's education.' It's always amazing to see how well this works in changing the parent's attitude. And from that point, we can actually talk to each other regarding the child. I've used this approach for years, and it works every time!"

And here's one of our favorites:

An effective teacher shared with us that she tells her students, on the very first day of school, "I just want you to know that if you do something inappropriate in this class, I will *not* write a note to your parents about it." The students breathe a sigh of relief. She then says, "Instead, you'll write the note. You're old enough now to understand that your parents need to know about certain things, but you're also old enough to write your own notes. You don't need for me to do that. Your parents would rather hear it straight from you anyway." Then, when a student does something wrong and the teacher feels a need to contact the parents about it, she simply has the student write a brief note to his parents explaining exactly he has done. The student signs it (with love, of course), and the teacher signs beneath that. The student then takes it home for a parent to sign. And on those occasions when a student "forgets" to return the signed note or to show the note to his parents, the teacher simply says, "Well, I wouldn't want for you to have to go through the trouble of writing another note, so let's just call your parent and you can explain what the note said." The teacher shared with us that the real beauty in this technique is that she never receives a call or a note from parents saying that their child says he didn't do what he was accused of doing. That's because the child actually admits, in the note, to exactly what it was he did! "In fact," she added, "the parents often call or write to apologize for what their child has done."

Remember that *your* attitude toward both children and their parents will help to determine the parents' attitudes toward you! Do you want parents on your side? Then convince them you're on their children's side!

Part 7.
How to Have the Best Attitude on the Faculty

Before you read on, ask yourself this question: "Who is the most positive person on my faculty?" Please don't read any further until you come up with someone's name. Okay, now for the really important question: Did you name yourself? If so, why? If not, why not?

Throughout this chapter (and throughout the book), we discuss the importance of a positive attitude about oneself and toward students, parents, coworkers, and others. **The most effective teachers know that to be as effective as they can be, they must portray a positive attitude.** They must be viewed by their students as happy people—the ones with the great attitudes.

Have you read any of the following books?

◆ *The Power of Negative Thinking*
◆ *How to Lose Friends and Aggravate People*
◆ *You Can't, So Don't Even Try*
◆ *A Losing Attitude Can Be Yours*
◆ *How to Experience the Failure You Deserve*

Well, have you? Of course you haven't. They don't exist, and most assuredly they never will. So what can you do so that you can always answer, "*Me!*" when asked who's the most positive person on your faculty? Here's the secret: *Be* the most positive person on your faculty. Take control of your attitude. Give your students what they so deserve—a positive role model! No, you can't control what other people do and who they are, but you can always be in control of yourself and of your attitude.

What do the most effective teachers do to ensure that their attitudes remain positive? Here's what a few had to say:

◆ "I don't really see it as a choice. I can't be effective without a positive attitude, and I want to be effective."
◆ "I know that the teachers who touched my life are the ones who had great attitudes, so I try to emulate their attitudes every day that I teach."
◆ "I really believe that a positive attitude is contagious. I do my best to spread mine around to both my students and my coworkers."
◆ "I encounter lots of students who don't have very positive attitudes, and I've learned that the more negative their attitudes are, the more

positive mine has to be. That's not always easy, but it works, so I do it!"

> One person really can make a difference—so be that one person. Shape up your attitude, and your students will remember you with gratitude!

Secret Four—Chapter Summary

Regarding attitude, remember the following:
- Attitude is everything!
- Find what's good, and focus on it. Find what's not so good, and make it better!
- Our attitudes help to shape the types of teachers, leaders, and role models we become.
- Don't gripe, groan, or gossip in the teachers' lounge or anywhere else.
- Your attitude and approach can either ignite a volatile situation or extinguish it.
- Portray an attitude of responsibility. Take your students' failures and successes personally.
- Burn calories by walking away from negative coworkers!
- Make positive contacts with parents.
- Convince a parent that you're on the side of his child by *being* on the side of his child!
- Have the best attitude on your faculty!

Secret Five

The Secret of Professionalism

Faculty Meeting

It was my first faculty meeting, and several teachers were talking

Talking while the principal spoke—gossiping and squawking

And then the issue of students arose, and those teachers ceased their balking

They said "Amen" to the issue of punishing students for too much talking

"Send them to the principal, remove them from my class

They're interfering with the learning of the others who want to pass

How dare they be so rude as to do the things they do!

They're embarrassing themselves, yet they do not have a clue

They speak when I am speaking, they don't do all their work

They obviously have no manners—responsibility they shirk!"

Well, as a brand-new teacher, I did not say a word

I just sat back and witnessed it all—the irony was absurd

How can you expect your students to do things you won't do?

If you want your students to be respectful, shouldn't it begin with you?

Part 1.
How and Why to Dress Professionally

If you walked through an airport, you would instantly be able to pick out, among the monstrous crowds, the pilots and the flight attendants. Are you psychic? Of course not. Or maybe you are, but you needn't be in this case. The pilots and flight attendants are professionally dressed in some type of uniform. You see, when you step onto an airplane, you want to feel that you're in capable, competent hands. But wouldn't the pilot be just as capable and competent if he were dressed in tennis shoes and blue jeans? Yes, he would, but the problem is that the passengers would not view him that way.

If you walked into a courtroom, could you pick out the attorneys? Yes, you could. Consider this: If you were accused of some awful crime that you did not commit, and on the day of your trial your attorney arrived in blue jeans and tennis shoes, you would immediately think to yourself, "I'm going to jail." Not because the attorney is any less competent, but rather because you would know that the jurors, the very ones who will determine your guilt or innocence, would not take him seriously. Like the pilot, the appropriately dressed attorney would look professional.

It has been proven, time and again, that the way we dress often influences the way others perceive us. Now let's take this idea into a school. There they are—hundreds of anxious, perceptive, role-model-seeking students just waiting to form perceptions of their teachers. And here come the teachers. How are they dressed? That depends. We guarantee you that you could not walk into any given school and immediately pick out all of the teachers because of their professional attire. Some you would recognize as teachers instantly. Others, we're afraid, would actually be dressed in blue jeans and tennis shoes! Okay, so does that make them any less competent? No. However, it definitely affects the ways their students perceive them, which inevitably affects their effectiveness.

If teaching truly is, as we believe, the noblest profession of all, then shouldn't all teachers dress the part? We believe they should. Now, does that mean that they have to go out, on their meager teacher salaries, and buy expensive clothing? Absolutely not. It does, however, mean that they should not dress like their students. If you're going to be on your feet all day, you can't be expected to wear high heels! But you can look professional! So here's a question to ask yourself each morning before you walk out of the house: "If a stranger were to meet me on the street, would he know that I am some type of professional?" If your answer is yes, then you are dressed professionally. If your answer is no, then go back to your closet and change—quickly—before the students see you!

The very best teachers, of course, know this secret. They act like professionals, they dress like professionals, and their students respect their professionalism. So take a good look at yourself.

> Does your attire leave something to be desired?

Part 2.
How to "Fit In" without "Falling In"

An interesting fact that we have observed is that the **very best teachers all manage to fit in without falling in.** We'll explain what we mean by that. In the most effective schools, there is a sense of family and teamwork. Yes, as in all families, there are a few who rock the boat at times. And within any school's family, some actually speak negatively about one another in the lounge. But for the most part, there is a sense of camaraderie and common purpose that makes for a positive school climate overall.

We also learned that when a teacher is new to a faculty, there is a dangerous chance that he or she may get caught up in the wrong circles by trying too hard to fit in. We call this *falling in.* And once you've fallen in, it's difficult to pull yourself out.

In our interviews with teachers, one teacher shared the following:

"I was a new teacher last year, and I made lots of mistakes in the classroom, but my biggest mistake was trying too hard to fit in with the faculty. I wanted everyone to like me, and before I knew it, I was hanging around the negative crowd way too much. But at the time, it felt good, because they were making me feel like any problem I was having was either because of the principal, the parents, or the students. Thank goodness a friend of mine who teaches at another school called my negative behaviors to my attention when she told me that I was starting to sound like the negative teachers on her faculty. This year is so much better. And though I'm still cordial to my last-year's 'support group,' I now associate with only those teachers who, I feel, can help me to become better and more positive."

In interviewing the most effective teachers, we learned the following, which we believe will help any teacher to fit in without falling in:

- ◆ Effective teachers are cordial to everyone.
- ◆ Effective teachers know the difference between friendly chitchat and gossip.
- ◆ Effective teachers politely excuse themselves from potentially explosive situations involving gossip or any type of unprofessional behaviors.
- ◆ Effective teachers maintain the privacy and dignity of their students.

- Effective teachers find solutions to the problems about which the less effective teachers are griping.
- Effective teachers never view themselves as victims.
- Effective teachers never attempt to fit in, and thus they never fall in. Rather, because of their professionalism and all of the things we mentioned above, they naturally fit in beautifully.

All of the effective teachers we interviewed agreed that fitting in was not something to which they ever gave much thought. They did admit, however, to knowing people who fell in while trying to fit in.

As one effective teacher put it:

> "If you do your job and you love kids and you serve as a good role model, you'll naturally fit in with all the others who do their jobs, who love kids, and who serve as role models. Hopefully, that's almost everyone on the faculty. As for the others, who would want to fit in with them anyway?"

Part 3.
How to Maintain Control of Your Actions

> ### Don't Let Us Know
>
> *When you get angry, and you will,*
> *Be careful and then more careful still*
> *Please don't let your anger show*
> *'Cause if you do, then we will know*
> *And once we know, that's it, you're through*
> *You belong to us, not us to you*
> *And once you're ours, we're in control*
> *We'll never do what we are told*
> *We'll push your buttons, we'll test your will*
> *We'll never ever get our fill*
> *So when you get angry, don't let it show*
> *'Cause if you do, then we will know*
> *And once we know, that's it, you're through*
> *You belong to us, not us to you.*

The most effective teachers know that the poem above is true. **If you let students know when they get to you** (and they *will* get to you), **then you have given your control over to them.** It is truly that simple. In Part 5 of this chapter, we talk about the fact that if you're going to call yourself a professional, then you have to act professionally at all times while practicing your profession. And losing your cool means losing your professionalism—period. In Part 7 of Secret Two, we discussed the infamous "screamers." Well, some teachers might not be screamers, but still they let their frustrations show and let the students see them sweat. This is a mistake.

So how do you avoid wearing your emotions on your sleeve? We asked this question of the most effective teachers, who, by the way, have this skill mastered. In summation, this is what they told us:

◆ The most effective teachers first recognize the importance of remaining in control of their actions and reactions with their students.

- Because they recognize the importance of being in control of themselves, they decide and actually commit, both to themselves and their students, to never, at any cost, lose their professionalism by losing control of their own emotions.
- The most effective teachers smile through the pain!
- The most effective teachers know how to be serious, and how to deal with serious misbehaviors, without being loud and losing control. In fact, the louder or more deviant a student is, the softer the effective teacher becomes.
- The most effective teachers pick and choose their battles. They don't get bent out of shape over every little student infraction.
- The most effective teachers never take student behavior personally.
- The most effective teachers attack the problem without ever attacking the person.
- The most effective teachers know how to fake it. In other words, even if they're boiling on the inside, they know how to look calm and cool on the outside.
- The most effective teachers know to think before they speak and that if they don't, they will almost always say something they'll later regret.
- The most effective teachers know that, sometimes, you have to turn away from the student, count to 10 or whatever number works, and compose yourself before you decide how to deal with a particular situation.
- The most effective teachers know that the only person who will look bad is the one who has lost control. Therefore, if a student loses his cool, he will be the only one who looks bad as long as the teacher doesn't do the same.
- The most effective teachers know how *not* to add fuel to a raging fire.
- And the most effective teachers know that you hold everything inside and then take it out on your spouse when you get home. Just kidding!

It is interesting to note that less effective teachers do the exact opposite of everything we have just listed. Is it any wonder they struggle, daily, with what they term "bad" students?

> So think before you act, and keep your emotions intact! Your students will be better behaved, and your sanity will be forever saved!

Part 4.
How and Why
to Continue Your Professional Growth

A Student Always

Doctors go to school
And then they get a degree
But we expect them to keep learning
So as teachers, why don't we?
How could we ever stop learning
Once we have a degree?
There's still so much to learn and do
To uncover and to see
So if I truly am the teacher
That I claim to be
Then I'm a student always
To teach, I have to be!

One of the main differences between effective teachers and less effective teachers is that **the most effective teachers never stop growing professionally.** They're constantly honing their skills and striving to be better in their teaching. Yes, some are striving for higher degrees and further certification, both of which can never be a waste. Even if you choose to stay in the classroom your entire career and never apply for any administrative positions, there's no such thing as an overqualified teacher. Just like medicine, teaching is not an exact science. As educators, we are constantly learning new and better ways of teaching. We haven't perfected it yet, and we're not ever likely to perfect it. But that's not why we better ourselves. We better ourselves to do just that—to better ourselves, to become even more skilled at what we do for as long as we do it.

You've heard the teachers who are literally counting the years, days, or even minutes until retirement. Imagine that you are about to undergo some serious type of surgery and you overhear your surgeon saying, "Hey, I know there's a better way to do this surgery, but I've only got one year left before I retire, and I'm sick and tired of going to these in-services!" Would you still allow this doctor to perform your operation, one that will affect your health for the rest of your life, *if* you survive the surgery? Of course you wouldn't! So why is it that for some reason we, as educators, just look the other way regarding ineffective teachers and actually count the years or days or minutes ourselves, until their retirement dates?

Now, you may be tempted to say that insisting that the less effective teachers better themselves is the job of administration, and that is a valid argument. In fact, it has been our experience that these teachers do only what they're forced to do regarding professional growth. However, the most effective teachers go above and beyond what is expected of them. This is not to say that you have to drive yourself to the point of insanity by constantly taking new courses, working on further certifications, and neglecting your home life. No, that's not at all what the most effective teachers do. Instead, they work consistently, steadily, and reasonably toward bettering themselves, one step at a time. And they do this because they see the value in it, not because their principals are making them go to yet another training session!

Okay, so another argument might be that you've been to tons of in-services where the presenters are boring. Again, this is a valid argument, as we all have been in that position at one time or another in our teaching careers. But the very best teachers know how to better themselves even in these types of situations. Here's what they do: They actually study the boring presenter and take note of what makes the presentation so bad. Then they do just the opposite in their classrooms. Yes, it's true that knowing what *not* to do is every bit as important as knowing what *to* do when presenting to a group of adults or when teaching a group of students in the classroom. The fact is that the only way to remain effective is to continue to learn to be effective! So attend anything you possibly can that will make you a better teacher.

Continue your learning—for truly you are a student always!

Part 5.
How to Bleed Professionalism
without Cutting Yourself

> ## I Bleed Professionalism
>
> *I bleed professionalism, yet I don't need medical attention*
> *The blood is not the red kind, but the kind of another dimension*
> *A dimension where I am a role model, and my blood spills onto*
> *   each student*
> *From me, I hope they will learn to be sensible, practical, prudent*
> *For everything I do and say is under their scrutiny*
> *Because everything I do and say influences who they will be*
> *My coworkers watch me also—I'm under a microscope*
> *They wait to see just how I'll react in a tough situation and cope*
> *So I'm careful about my words, my dress, and the look upon my face*
> *One's professionalism or lack of it can make or break a place!*

The above poem summarizes what the best teachers are all about. They bleed professionalism—and though it's not in any way medically detrimental, it's psychologically not always an easy thing to do. It can be so tempting to "fall in," as we discussed earlier in Part 2 (page 82) of this chapter. Teaching can be frustrating, and it's often tempting to share those frustrations with others. That's why the teachers' lounge is never a dull place! Frustrations abound, and they always tend to land there. So what happens if you let it out—if you just lose it every now and then? We'll tell you what happens. If you lose it, you've lost it. You've lost your professionalism and thus the respect of other professionals. And once you've lost it, getting it back is difficult. A much better solution is to just hang on to your professionalism, at all costs, in the first place. **Don't allow your frustrations to rob you of your dignity and your professionalism, regardless of how tempting it may be.**

Ms. Professional had been teaching many years. However, it was her first year teaching at this particular school. On her very first day, she was greeted enthusiastically by Ms. WarnYa. Ms. WarnYa was the self-appointed hostess who warned everyone of the awful students who inhabited the school. She quickly accosted Ms. Professional, looked at her class list, and began offering intricate details of the bad students' backgrounds, family lives, grooming habits (or lack thereof), previous infractions, and so on. She was a true font of information—the kind of information that can only harm others. Ms. WarnYa had an identical twin in Ms. Professional's previous school, and Ms. Professional recognized the resemblance right away and said the following, which, we might add, was a stroke of genius, or, at the very least, pure professionalism: "Thank you so much, Ms. WarnYa, for pointing out those four students to me. It seems that you've taken quite an interest in their well-being. You know, I became a teacher, as I'm sure you did also, because of the students you just pointed out to me, because those are the ones who need me the most. So I promise that I'll be extra kind and attentive to those students. And once again, thanks so much for caring enough to let me know!"

Was that great or what? Needless to say, Ms. WarnYa walked away from that conversation in a daze. And that, teachers, is what the best teachers do regarding professionalism. They bleed it! No matter what others say and do, and no matter how frustrated they may become at times, they know and live by the following:

> If you're going to *call* yourself a professional, then you have to *act* professionally at all times while practicing your profession!

Part 6.
How to *Do* Your Best, Not *Be* the Best

Here's a test question for you: Who was the greatest classroom teacher of all time? Do you know? Neither do we. Neither does anyone for that matter. And does it really matter? You see, teaching is not a contest. There's no prize for being the best. **The true prize in teaching comes from touching a student's life.** And you do that by doing your absolute best, being your absolute best, and giving your absolute best every day that you teach. That's it. Sounds simple? Think again.

The most effective teachers know that doing their best is not easy. In fact, it's quite difficult. It's actually exhausting. It takes hard work, dedication, patience, determination, and much more. In Part 4 (page 86) of this chapter, we discussed the importance of continuing your professional growth throughout your teaching career. This is part of doing your best.

We asked several effective teachers to share their secrets for maintaining their positive attitudes, continuing to grow professionally, maintaining high levels of enthusiasm, and, overall, doing their best on a continual basis. Here are some of their actual quotes:

- ◆ "If you're going to call yourself a true teacher, then you must be constantly on your toes, always appear enthusiastic—even when you don't feel like it—and continue to learn new and better ways of doing things. It's tiring, but it's also rewarding. It's all for the children. And if you can keep that as your main focus, you're going to make a difference."

- ◆ "I'm a role model for every student I teach. So it's not an option to slack off at any time during the school day. I've got to be aware, constantly, that everything I say and do has a profound impact on my students. It's such a tremendous responsibility."

- ◆ "I never try to be the best. I'm not competing with anyone. I simply try to do my best every day that I teach."

- ◆ "I feel as though every day that I teach is a new adventure. In teaching, you never know what each day—or each moment, for that matter—will bring. You have to be ready for whatever the students throw at you. And believe me, they do throw. But instead of playing the part of 'catcher,' I consider myself more of a coach. I really believe that if you can remind yourself, every day, of the impact that you have on these students' lives, then you can't help but learn and grow as a teacher. Anything less would mean cheating the students of the quality education they so deserve."

♦ "I never think of teaching as a job. Rather, I consider it a privilege. To be able to see those young eyes light up when they learn something new, to hear their youthful laughter, and to know that you're a part of that learning and laughter is the most rewarding feeling in the world. The children give me the energy I need to do my best every day."

♦ "I think the secret is that you have to love children. Sadly, there are some teachers who consider the students aggravations and necessary evils that at least provide them with a paycheck. I can't imagine doing something I don't love. And teaching children is something I absolutely love. So how can I possibly give them anything but my very best?"

♦ "There's so much to learn about teaching, and I don't think you can ever learn it all. I, for one, after 32 years of teaching, feel that I have barely scratched the surface of all there is to know about teaching. But the secret is to just keep learning at least one new thing every day that you teach. Also, ask lots of questions of your coworkers. I'm constantly bugging my coworkers, trying to get new ideas. They don't mind, of course. After all, they're teachers!"

We simply cannot add to that. They've managed to say it all!

Part 7.
How to Make Decisions That Benefit Children

While writing this book, we compared two schools that were similar in size, population, demographics, and so on. The only difference was the quality of the teachers. One school had a reputation of having very effective teachers, and the other had the opposite reputation. Not surprisingly, the achievement levels of the students were dramatically different from one school to the next. (We won't insult your intelligence by telling you which school had higher achievement!) So we took a closer look, and summarized below is what we found:

- Teachers in the more effective school were much more positive in their demeanors, in the ways they spoke of their school, in the ways they spoke of one another, and, of course, in the ways they treated children.

- Teachers in the more effective school wrote detailed lesson plans, whereas in the less effective school, lesson plans consisted of simple checklists that basically gave no information other than on what page in the textbook the activity could be found, along with, of course, the page numbers of the worksheets.

- Teachers in the more effective school used textbooks as resources, whereas teachers in the less effective school relied solely on textbooks for their curriculum.

- Teachers in the more effective school, though they spent time each day planning together, were not all on the same textbook page on the same day. They taught according to the needs of their students. Teachers in the less effective school, however, were all on the same textbook page every day. If the students got it, good. If they didn't, tough.

- Assessment methods were drastically different from one school to the other. In the more effective school, assessments were authentic, whereby students actually showed their work, proved their points, and demonstrated their thinking on tests. In the less effective school, assessments consisted almost solely of true–false, multiple-choice, and fill-in-the-blank type questions. These, the teachers admitted, were less time-consuming and easier to grade.

- In the more effective school, writing was taught across the curriculum. In the less effective school, writing was reserved for the language arts teacher.
- Teachers in the more effective school continued to receive training in effective teaching techniques, whereas teachers in the less effective school jumped from program to program hoping to find a quick fix.
- Teachers in the more effective school knew their students—every one of them. Teachers in the less effective school knew very little about their students. The second group agreed, however, that the students were bad.
- Teachers in the more effective school spent much more time actually teaching than in the less effective school, where the approach was more mechanical (lecture, read the chapter, answer the questions at the end of the chapter, complete the worksheets, define the vocabulary words, etc.)
- Teachers in the more effective school dealt with discipline problems in a calm, controlled manner and usually handled discipline problems on their own. Teachers in the less effective school lost their cool a lot and frequently relied on the office to handle their discipline problems for them.
- The less effective school had more than five times the discipline referrals than the more effective school. Surprised?

In interviewing the teachers of both schools, we noted that one thing was blatantly different. The teachers in the more effective school all agreed that children were the main priority and that they were willing to put in more work and do whatever it took to do what was best for each child in the school. Not one teacher from the less effective school stated that children were a priority. Not one! Most of the teachers in the less effective school complained about their students and made excuses for why the test scores were so low. They also complained about parents, administration, the school board—you name it.

The bottom line was that we found that the teachers in the more effective school applied the seven simple secrets every day. The teachers in the less effective school did not. And the absolute bottom line was that the **teachers in the more effective school made *all* decisions based on what was best for students,** as opposed to what was easiest for teachers!

So how do you ensure that you're making all of your decisions based on what's best for students instead of on what's easiest for you, the teacher? Very simply. You do the following: With every decision you make, ask yourself, every time, "Is this what's best for my students or what's easiest for me?" That's it!

If you make decisions based on the children you teach, mountains they will climb for you; stars they will reach!

Secret Five—Chapter Summary

Regarding professionalism, remember the following:

- If you're going to call yourself a professional, then you have to appear professional at all times when practicing your profession. (We know we've said this three times thus far, but we feel it's just that important!)
- Dress such that your students will see you as a professional and that anyone you meet will instantly know you're a professional.
- If you try too hard to fit in, you're more than likely to fall in.
- Once you've fallen in, no one offers a hand to pull you out!
- Remain in control of your actions and reactions with students, no matter what.
- Do not take student behavior personally.
- You can be serious without being loud and losing control.
- Always attack the problem; never attack the person.
- Never stop growing professionally.
- There's no such thing as an overqualified teacher.
- Bleed professionalism!
- Do your best, be your best, and give your best every day that you teach.
- Keep your students as your main focus. Make *every* decision based on what's best for them, as opposed to what's easiest for you.

Secret Six

The Secret of Effective Discipline

Pushing My Buttons

I pushed the little button to summon the elevator

Since I was in a hurry, I needed it sooner, not later

I waited and waited and waited for the elevator to arrive

I pushed the button once, then twice—then three times, four times, five

But it never did arrive, you see, and so I took the stairs

A better source of exercise for anyone who dares

And then I got to thinking of the students in my class

Pushing my buttons every day, pushing hard and fast

And there I go reacting, and their "elevator" arrives

They're riding up, they're riding down, and I'm the one with hives

I wonder if I stopped arriving, if they'd have to take the stairs

I could silence their conniving—the answer to my prayers!

And so I'll start tomorrow; my buttons I will hide

And when they see I won't react, another they'll try to ride

So here's advice to all of you, the teachers who react

Don't let them know your buttons work; they'll stop pushing—
*   that's a fact!*

Part 1.
How to Hide Your Buttons from Your Students

Have you ever found yourself waiting for an elevator and pushing the button more than once? Did you really think it would come faster if you pushed the button repeatedly? Did it? Of course not. (Imagine, if that really *did* work, the poor people inside the elevator zooming at breakneck speed because of some impatient person pushing the button repeatedly!) Well, if the elevator had not come, what would you have done? Taken the stairs, right? Or, at the very least, you would have sought another elevator. And that's exactly what students do in the classroom. Students push our buttons. First, they push once. The most effective teachers, of course, do not react. So the students push again, sometimes harder and faster. You see, they're trying desperately to make the teacher react—not because they're bad, but because they're children.

Less effective teachers fall for it every time. They react immediately! And so the students continue to push the buttons of these teachers, and they ride these teachers all year long. And all year long, these teachers complain that they've once again been given the worst students in the school. How could this happen to them yet again? Well, there's a simple solution, and the most effective teachers know it. They hide their buttons. The secret of hiding their buttons from their students is that they simply don't react—at least not on the outside. That's not to say they don't get aggravated and that they don't feel like reacting. Of course they do. They're every bit as human as the less effective teachers.

Think of it this way: Imagine that you go to a set of elevators and there are no buttons. What would you do? You would probably find yourself feeling quite confused, so you would continue to search the same wall over and over, thinking that there surely must be a button somewhere. But once you realized that there simply is no button, you would have to take the stairs or find another set of elevators. Once again, this is a good analogy of what occurs in the classrooms of the most effective teachers. Yes, students will try to find your buttons. They will continue to search if your buttons are not readily apparent. But soon enough, they will give up and go to some other poor, unsuspecting teacher down the hall who has clearly marked buttons—the kind that are lighted and flashing, complete with sirens!

So how do you stop students from pushing your buttons? You start with an awareness that your students actually *are* pushing your buttons. Here are a few simple questions to ask yourself to determine if your buttons are being pushed:

- Do the students know when they get to me?
- Can they tell that I am aggravated?
- What do I look like when I get aggravated, upset, or frustrated with my students?

If you can honestly answer those questions, then you are now aware of what *not* to do from here on out. Instead, do just the opposite. If you normally sigh, don't. Just take a moment to breathe and be consciously aware of appearing calm. If you normally raise your voice in anger or frustration, do just the opposite. Speak slowly and softly, albeit in a serious tone, as you can hold a student accountable without losing your patience. And remember that if you're so mad you can't think straight, you're right—you can't think straight. So don't take any action until you *can* think straight. You can do it!

> Here's the secret: Appearing calm is the best balm for soothing a situation without showing frustration.

Part 2.
How to Be Consistent with Discipline

One of the best-kept secrets of the very best teachers is that they have *very* few discipline problems. They do, of course, have discipline challenges. You see, as long as there are students, there will always be discipline challenges. But the very best teachers never allow those challenges to become problems. We found that they have two simple things in common:

- They have a very specific discipline plan.
- They enforce the discipline plan consistently.

Sounds simple? It is. These teachers, we have learned, do not complicate things. They begin by establishing a plan. The plan includes only a few rules. Each rule has a consequence—a very definite, specific, and appropriate consequence—if it is broken. The students know this up front, and they know they can count on the teacher to follow that plan no matter what. Consistency, consistency, consistency!

One teacher put it this way: "Students want rules. They want to know exactly what they can and can't do in any teacher's classroom. So I tell them up front, and I let them know that since I'm a person of my word, then I will always follow the discipline plan. I actually convince them that *they* have come up with the plan. Then, when a student breaks a rule, he knows exactly what the consequence will be, and I never get bent out of shape over it. I simply remind him that he chose to break a rule, and thus there is a consequence. It saves me so much stress and heartache. I refuse to 'argue' or 'bargain' with my students. They need to know that I'm a professional, I'm in charge, and I'm consistent."

Another teacher shared the following: "I have only four rules, but I'm very consistent with them. The key, however, is that I'm very calm when I enforce them. One of my rules is that no student is allowed to tease another student. I explain exactly what I mean by 'teasing' and I tell them that I care about each of them way too much to allow anyone to tease them. In other words, I 'have their backs.' When a student does tease another, and it does happen occasionally, I calmly dole out the consequence. No fussing, no arguing, no stress. It works, as I have very few discipline problems, regardless of the students I teach. Everyone wonders how I manage it, and I tell them exactly what I do. I'm always amazed that more teachers don't just do what I do!"

In observing both of the afore-mentioned teachers, along with many others we consider the very best, we also discovered that they were excellent classroom managers. And as discussed in Secret 2, Parts 2 and 3, teachers who have good management plans have very few rules, as they rely much more on procedures. Their rules, though few, are enforced consistently.

So we encourage you to do what the very best teachers do—**have a discipline plan and be consistent with it.** Don't argue with students when they break rules. There's no need to argue with a student *ever!*

Bottom line?

> If a rule is broken, no harsh words need be spoken. Just set your rules and be consistent, and discipline problems will be almost nonexistent!

Part 3.
How to Relieve Stress with Psychology

It's no secret, or maybe it is, that **the very best teachers are the ones who seem the least stressed and have the fewest discipline problems.** This is because they know how to use good psychology to ward off potential problems, and the best part is that they actually have fun doing it.

Below are two examples of some of these teachers having fun with psychology:

Example 1

Ms. "Brightside" (That's not her name but it should be!) had a student who was sewing, yes, sewing, in class. She was mending the strap on her denim purse. Instead of singling the student out and embarrassing her by punishing her or saying something like, "Monica, put that away right now or you'll go to the office!" Ms. Brightside, with a smile on her face, quietly went to Monica and said, "Monica, I had no idea you were so talented. I know you know you'll have to put it up, but it's good to know that you can sew. I'd love to learn to sew. In fact, I've got a jacket that needs a button sewn on it. If I brought it to you, do you think you could fix it for me?" The student, shocked, quickly put her sewing away and nodded that she would fix Ms. Brightside's jacket. The best part is that Ms. Brightside admitted to us that she actually went home, removed a button from one of her jackets, and brought the jacket to Monica. Monica took the jacket home and returned it, button expertly sewn, the very next day. "She's been nothing but helpful and attentive ever since!" said Ms. Brightside with a chuckle.

When asked why she used this particular technique with Monica, Ms. Brightside said, "She's a troubled child with a lot of problems both at home and at school. I knew that scolding her and embarrassing her in front of her peers would only breed resentment, which would lead to things much worse than sewing, which would lead to more fussing, and the vicious cycle would continue. So, instead, I used a little psychology. I'm thinking of having her make a new outfit for me!"

Example 2

A very effective teacher told us that he discovered that *all* students like to run errands or do a favor for the teacher. So when he has a student who is not working—for whatever reason—he simply says to the student, "As soon as you finish your work, I need you to do something for me. So let me know as soon as you finish. Thanks." He says it never fails. The student gets busy immediately. And then the teacher actually gets to praise the student for working so well. Sometimes he will simply have the student get something for him from across the room. Other times, he will have the student deliver something to the office. "I literally trick them into working," he says. "It's great fun, and the students don't even know I'm doing it! Besides that, I know that if I get into power struggles with my students by using my 'authority' or my 'teacher eye' to get them to do their work, I'm in for big discipline problems. I actually believe that I avoid probably 90% of the discipline problems I would have if I didn't use good psychology with my students."

These, of course, are just two of many ways to have fun with psychology to ensure fewer discipline problems. We continue to find that the very best teachers use what they know about the psychology of working with children to get their students to work hard, behave well, and achieve. We also continue to find that teachers who understand how to use psychology are often heard using similar phrases in their classrooms. Here are a few of those phrases:

- Thank you for…
- I really appreciate…
- I trust that you….
- I understand…
- I like the way you….
- I'm very proud of you for…
- You must be proud of yourself for…

And our very favorite phrase is this: "What in the world did I do to deserve this wonderful class?"

> Psychology works, and it's lots of fun. Use it, lest you come undone.

Part 4. How to Become Better, Not Bitter

In our observations, we came across a few—okay, maybe a little more than a few—teachers we would consider bitter. In talking to these teachers, we began to notice some similarities. Below are a few typical phrases from these teachers:

- ◆ I'm counting the days until retirement!
- ◆ If I could just get rid of three students, my life would be heaven!
- ◆ I send the bad kids to the administrator, but the administrator never does anything.
- ◆ Kids today! You just can't motivate them.
- ◆ Their parents don't care, so how am I supposed to reach them?
- ◆ I'm sick of the paperwork! When am I supposed to find time to teach?
- ◆ The students don't care. They're lazy.

Okay, so we've established what bitterness sounds like, just in case you've never heard it in your own school. The sad fact is that these teachers don't know that there's a better way because they've fallen into a bitter way.

Take a look around your own school, and you'll notice that **the very best teachers always choose the better, as opposed to the bitter, path.** When a student misbehaves in the classroom of an effective teacher, here's what usually happens:

- ◆ The teacher acts instead of reacts.
- ◆ The teacher speaks to the student in a calm manner.
- ◆ The teacher tries to find out what caused the misbehavior by talking to the student.
- ◆ The teacher treats the student with dignity, at the same time holding the student accountable for his actions.
- ◆ The teacher never loses his cool.

The bottom line is that the very best teachers use every situation—even the negative ones—to help themselves become better at what they do. You see, the very best teachers, just like the less effective teachers, experience frustrations. They make mistakes. They teach the *same* students. The difference is that they choose to turn each of these situations into productive learning opportunities, as opposed to falling victim to themselves!

Secret 6. Part 4.

Think of it this way:

◆ Would you prefer a better doctor or a bitter doctor?

◆ Would you prefer a better financial advisor or a bitter financial advisor?

◆ Would you prefer a better spouse or a bitter spouse?

◆ Would you prefer better milk or bitter milk?

Just as bitter milk leaves a bad taste in your mouth, bitter teachers leave a bad memory in the minds of their students.

> *Would you agree that better butter*
> *Tastes better than bitter butter?*
> *And have you noticed that bitter teachers*
> *Never seem to utter*
> *A positive word about anything*
> *Or anyone for that matter?*
> *A bitter teacher or better teacher?*
> *I'll always choose the latter!*

Part 5.
How to Give Students
What They Want and Need

The very best teachers shared a secret with us. Here it is: **If you want to know what a student wants and needs, ask him!**

So we took them up on that. We went to the students, and we asked them what the ideal teacher would be like. We interviewed students from kindergarten through 12th grade, and we were not surprised to see that their answers were remarkably similar. Below is a summary of what the students told us they wanted and needed from their teachers:

- Students want teachers to be nice and smile often.
- Students want teachers to care about them.
- Students want teachers to be understanding.
- Students want teachers to help them when they are struggling.
- Students want teachers to be patient with them.
- Students want teachers to be fair and consistent.
- Students want teachers who actually like teaching.
- Students want teachers they can trust.
- Students want teachers who don't scream at them.
- Students want teachers who actually get to know them.
- Students want teachers who believe in them.
- Students want teachers who make learning interesting and meaningful.
- Students want teachers who don't embarrass them in front of their peers.
- Students want teachers who challenge them to be their best.
- Students want teachers who help them succeed.
- Students want teachers who don't give up on them.

The list goes on, but you get the point. It is surprising to find that many teachers never ask their students what they want, need, and expect to gain from the class. And, not surprisingly, those are the teachers with the most discipline problems.

If you ask your own students what they want and need from you, you're sure to hear the same things listed above. But ask them anyway, as it shows that you actually care about and listen to your students. That is not to say that you can ever accommodate every child's wants and needs. That's not realistic. But you can definitely be the teacher listed above. And just for the fun of it, interview a 5-year-old and an 18-year-old. You'll be amazed at how similar their answers are.

Okay, so now that we've established what students want and need, the rest is completely up to you. A good idea might be to take that list and change it slightly, turning it into your own Teacher's Creed that you proudly display in your classroom. It might look like this:

My Promises to You, My Students:

I promise to be nice and smile often.

I promise to care about each of you.

I promise to be understanding.

I promise to help you when you are struggling.

I promise to be patient with you.

I promise to be fair and consistent.

I promise to enjoy teaching you.

I promise to be trustworthy.

I promise never to scream at you.

I promise that I will get to know you.

I promise to believe in you.

I promise to make learning interesting and meaningful.

I promise that I will not embarrass you in front of your peers.

I promise that I will challenge you to be your very best.

I promise to do everything I can to help you succeed.

And I promise that, no matter what, I will never give up on you.

Be the teacher that every child wants and deserves. That kind of classroom calms everyone's nerves!

Part 6.
How to Be Self-Disciplined

One common trait of all effective teachers is self-discipline. Why is this so important in the classroom? It's important because **if you can't control yourself, you'll never control a group of students.** Therefore, self-discipline is a priority.

Follow us into the classrooms of two teachers who handle the same situation with noticeably different approaches. One possesses self discipline. The other does not.

First, we'll observe the classroom of Ms. Fuse Box.

Ms. Fuse Box

Amy is not doing her work, and Ms. Fuse Box tells her to get busy. Amy snaps at Ms. Fuse Box by saying, "I'm not doing anything, you b****. (You may or may not choose to fill in the expletive.)

Ms. Fuse Box stops, stares at Amy with her meanest teacher eye, and says, "What did you just say?" So, of course, Amy answers Ms. Fuse Box's question by telling her, yet again, what she just said. Ms. Fuse Box ignites and explodes. Amy fuels the fire. The flames soon envelop them both. Amy is then written up and sent to the office. Ms. Fuse Box angrily continues her lesson and continues to burn with rage for the rest of the day. And Amy is quietly planning her revenge as she waits to see the principal. Thank goodness Ms. Fuse Box does not have a cat, because she would kick it when she arrived home. Instead, she'll kick Mr. Fuse Box.

And now, on to the classroom of Ms. Rattleless.

Ms. Rattleless

Amy is not doing her work, and Ms. Rattleless tells her to get busy. Amy snaps at Ms. Rattleless by saying, "I'm not doing anything, you b****. (By now, you've figured out the expletive.)

Ms. Rattleless stops and calmly says to Amy, "I can tell you're really upset right now. I'll talk to you when you calm down." And Ms. Rattleless continues teaching the class as if nothing has happened. Amy is both defused and confused, as she was hoping for a power struggle. Later, Ms. Rattleless walks into the hall with Amy and says, "Amy, what happened? It seems as if you got so frustrated you just snapped! I felt so bad for you. That must have been awful. Is there something bothering you?" Amy tells Ms. Rattleless that she had an argument with her mother before coming to school and is upset. She then apologizes to Ms. Rattleless. The teacher and student return to the classroom.

Now let's analyze these two scenarios:

- Ms. Fuse Box allowed her buttons to be pushed by Amy.
- Ms. Rattleless did not allow her buttons to be pushed by Amy.
- Both teachers were initially shocked, but Ms. Fuse Box reacted, whereas Ms. Rattleless acted.
- Ms. Fuse Box lost control of herself.
- Ms. Rattleless remained in control of herself.
- Ms. Fuse Box added fuel to Amy's fire.
- Ms. Rattleless did *not* add fuel to Amy's fire.
- Ms. Fuse Box acted personally insulted.
- Ms. Rattleless acted personally concerned.

The best teachers know that, no matter what, losing self-control is not an option. The fact is that, in every classroom, someone will always be in control. Will it be you or your students?

> When you lose control, that's it, you're through. You belong to your students, not they to you!

Part 7.
How to Find the Good in Every Child

The old saying "People do better when they feel better" holds true in the classroom, and the most effective teachers use this concept to their benefit. The best teachers know that **children who feel good about themselves are much less likely to misbehave than ones who do not.** So how do you make children feel good about themselves? You find something good about them and praise it. That's it. But what if you simply cannot find anything good about a particular student? Then open your eyes. There's good in every child.

As teachers, we've been trained to identify problems, diagnose what's causing the problems, and then find solutions to those problems. That's a good thing, unless, of course, you focus solely on problems. You then become one of the bitter teachers we discussed in Part 4 (page 102) of this chapter. The fact remains that teachers tend to be better at identifying what's wrong with students than they are at identifying what's right.

Do you remember taking courses in college about identifying learning and/or behavior problems, along with learning techniques to address those problems? We all took those courses, and they were necessary and useful. But do you remember taking courses about identifying good behavior and student success and techniques for fostering those behaviors and successes? No, you do not remember taking those courses, because, sadly, those courses are not offered. However, **the most effective teachers,** despite not having taken such courses, **are adept at finding what's good in every student.** They constantly identify and encourage good behavior in students, which, of course, guarantees even more good behavior.

One effective teacher shared the following with us: "The first and most important thing I do each year is to get to know as much as I can about my students—their interests, their talents, their hobbies, etc. I just use a simple interest inventory to do this, and, of course, I talk to my students a lot. My students get to know me and I get to know them on a personal level. I'm always amazed at the talents of my students—some are artists, some are musicians, some are mechanics, some are scholars, some are philosophers, etc., but *all* are talented. Some just don't know their potential, and it is my privilege to help them attain it!"

Another teacher we observed uses what she calls the "thank you" technique. Here's how it works: She consciously uses the words *thank you* many times each day, from the time students enter the room until the time they leave. She actually thanks them for coming to class as she greets them at the door each day. She thanks them for following procedures. She thanks a student who enters the classroom obviously upset about something that happened at recess by saying: "Thank you for not bringing in any frustrations from recess. I can tell you're upset, and I know how difficult it must be not to bring that attitude into the classroom. So I just wanted to say thanks in advance for not doing that. I really appreciate it." That, teachers, is called being proactive and noticing the good things that students do and the good people that they can be.

No great teacher sees students as they really are, but rather as the people they can become. There really is much good inside of every child, but sometimes you have to dig deep to find what's not on the surface.

> So take out your shovels if you must
> Remove the cobwebs and the dust
> You'll be amazed at what you find
> There's good inside each heart and mind.

Secret Six—Chapter Summary

Regarding discipline, remember the following:
- Do not allow your students to see your buttons. If they can't see them, they can't push them.
- Appear calm in any situation.
- Have a very specific discipline plan.
- Enforce your discipline plan consistently.
- Never argue or bargain with a student.
- If you have well-established procedures in place, you'll need very few rules.
- Use clever psychology to ward off potential discipline problems.
- Ask students what they want, need, and expect from your class.
- Establish a Teacher's Creed and post it.
- Use every situation to learn and grow as a teacher. Remember to focus on becoming better, not bitter.

- Attack the problem, not the person.
- Never lose your cool with a student.
- Practice self-discipline. Don't allow yourself to become a Ms. Fuse Box.
- Find the good in every child.
- Find the good in every child.
- Find the good in every child. (We felt that that one was worth repeating!)

Secret Seven

The Secret of Motivation and Inspiration

An Ounce of Inspiration

Give me an ounce of inspiration
Leading, of course, to motivation
Which will spark my imagination
Thus you'll see my perspiration
As I feel my mind's vibration
Spurring on my new creation
Concentration for the duration
Whew! I did it! Pure elation!

Part 1.
How to Make *Your* Excitement
Their Excitement

It is often said that **we remember two groups of teachers—the really good ones, and, of course, the really bad ones!**

Please take a moment to reflect on the best teacher you ever had. You'll probably be amazed at how much you can recall about that classroom. You may be able to remember some of the students, what the room looked like, one or more exciting activities or events that occurred, and possibly even some of the daily routines. But even if you are not able to recall any of that, you will surely be able to recall how you *felt* in that classroom. And more than anything, you remember the teacher—the teacher who brought joy and happiness and success into your life, the same teacher you still carry in your heart as you read these pages.

Now we'll suffer along with you as you reflect on the worst teacher you ever had. Can't you still *feel* it? The way you and other students were treated? The way you felt in the presence of that teacher? The awful tone that the teacher brought to class each day? The dreaded sound of that teacher's voice?

Okay, sorry about that. We didn't mean to raise your blood pressure, but we wanted to make a point. All of us had classes that we loved and those we dreaded. And that love or dread factor was determined by one person—the teacher! It is not surprising that **in the classrooms of the very best teachers, the excitement is contagious.** As one effective teacher put it:

"As a teacher, my mood sets the weather in the classroom each day. My tone establishes the tone for the entire class. If I look out at my students and see an uninspired group, my next glance is in the mirror. Though it's not always easy, I know that in order to motivate and inspire my students, I have to be motivated and inspired *first*. So, on those days when I'm not feeling so motivated and enthusiastic, I just pretend to be. My students don't know the difference!"

On a daily basis, we meet and greet our fellow teachers and other coworkers at school. And every time a coworker asks how we're doing, we have a choice. If we smile and say, "Great! How are you?" then that sets a positive tone. If we respond by saying, "Do you *really* want to know?" that sets a completely different tone. The fact remains that as teachers, as human beings, we all have personal issues—some good and some not. So here's a secret:

Less effective teachers bring their personal problems and resulting moods into their classrooms. Effective teachers do not!

Every day, both effective and ineffective teachers make decisions on how they will approach the day. The effective teachers see the glass as half full, the less effective teachers see the glass as half empty, and the worst of the bunch see it as just another dirty glass to wash!

Students respond best to enthusiastic, highly motivated teachers. If the teacher can convince the students that he or she sees the lesson as relevant, motivating, and exciting, the students are much more likely to see the lesson as relevant, motivating, and exciting. Approach is everything. The very best teachers can take seemingly boring content and bring it to life. Less effective teachers can kill even the most exciting content.

Bottom line? It's up to you. You choose your attitude every day in the classroom. Students then take their cues from you. You create the weather.

What's tomorrow's forecast in your classroom? Clear and sunny, cloudy with a chance of storms, or severe thunderstorms with heavy downpours and possible tornadoes?

Part 2. How to Make Every Student Feel Like Your Favorite Student

Secret 7. Part 2.

If you walked into the classrooms of the most effective teachers and could get inside the minds of their students, you would find that every one of the students secretly thinks he or she is the teacher's favorite student. Conversely, if you walked into the classrooms of the least effective teachers and could get inside the minds of their students, you would find that all of the students do *not* feel like the teacher's favorite, because these teachers have particular favorite students—usually one or two—and, yes, these particular students are highly resented by the other students. These are the ones the other students refer to as the teacher's pets. That, by the way, is never a good thing. **All students want and deserve to feel just as valued as every other student in the classroom.** The most effective teachers know this, so they find ways to make each student feel special and valued.

When asked about how it was possible to make all students feel equally valued, here is what one effective teacher had to say:

"I know that when a student feels like he's special to me, then he's much more likely to behave, to do his work, and to enjoy learning. If I can get a student to behave, to do his work, and to enjoy learning, then there's practically nothing I can't teach him. So if I want all of my students to behave, do their work, and enjoy learning, I've simply got no choice but to make them all feel like they're special to me. I go out of my way every day to be courteous, to welcome them into my classroom, to listen to them, to get to know something personal about them, to cheer them on when they succeed, and to encourage them when they're struggling. It doesn't mean I don't hold my students accountable. I do! But I treat them all with the same dignity and respect with which my favorite teacher treated me. I really thought I was her favorite student. But come to think of it, so did all of the other students!"

The most effective teachers know that if every student in the class feels valued, then none of them will resent the other students being valued. However, if some students do not feel that sense of worthiness in the classroom, then the classroom becomes a breeding ground for resentment.

We continue to notice that the most effective teachers are adept at making generalized positive comments. Here's an example: The students reenter the classroom after lunch and the teacher, in a friendly, positive tone, says, "Thank you for walking into the room so quietly. I really appreciate how quickly you're getting ready for class." As this is said in a sincere manner, do you know which students think the teacher is talking about them? All the ones who were doing what she just praised. This is known as anonymous public praise, and it works. In doing this, the teacher is teaching the students what's important to her and what she expects from them. She's also making all of her students feel important and valued, because even the students who might not have been quiet upon entering the room are wondering if it's possible that maybe she didn't see them, and they usually get quiet and busy following the teacher's praise.

Now let's contrast this with the teacher who yells, "Be quiet!" Even if only a few students were not being quiet, this teacher has just used anonymous public fussing, and it doesn't work. She just treated all students as though they were behaving inappropriately, even the ones who were behaving. And the students who are the most affected are the ones who weren't even talking in the first place. It's sort of like when the principal makes an announcement saying, "Some teachers have still not turned in their grades!" Even, and especially, the teachers who have already turned in their grades race to the office, gasping for breath, asking the secretary, "Have I not turned in my grades yet? Luckily, I made five backup copies, and one of them is at home in the refrigerator, just in case we have a house fire!" The teachers, of course, who have not yet turned in their grades are the least bothered by it all. In fact, the anonymous public fussing just led them to think, "Oh, good, it's not just me who's late. There's a whole bunch of us!"

Though we will address the use of praise more specifically in Part 4 of this chapter, we wanted to make the point here that the effective use of anonymous public praise helps to make all students feel valued. Anonymous public fussing accomplishes the opposite. Students who feel equally valued are secretly convinced that they are the teacher's favorite student. Want to motivate and inspire your students? Convince them each one is your favorite.

Who's My Teacher's Favorite?

Who's my teacher's favorite?
I'm pretty sure it's me
What? You think it's you instead?
That simply cannot be!
Of course, now that you mention it
She treats us both the same
She smiles at me, she smiles at you
She calls us both by name
She helps me when I'm struggling
She does the same with you
She helps us to be better
At whatever we're trying to do
With any classroom rule she has
She makes us both comply
And when we feel like giving up,
She encourages us to try
So who's her favorite student, then?
We simply can't deny
That unmistakably, unequivocally
It seems to be a tie!

Part 3.
How to Show a Personal
Interest in Every Student

Effective teachers will all agree that **one of the best ways to motivate and inspire students is to show personal interest in them.** Less effective teachers don't take the time to get to know their students. They just don't see the point in it.

A curriculum supervisor was called into a teacher's classroom at the request of the teacher. According to the teacher, one particular student was causing nothing but trouble. This teacher claimed to have tried *everything*, but the student simply would not behave. Upon observing this teacher's class, the supervisor noticed two things instantly: (1) the student was seated all the way in the back of the room—and, of course, the teacher never left the front of the room, and (2) the student had a large cast on his leg.

Following the observation, the teacher said to the supervisor, "Well, of course he behaved today because you were here." The supervisor then asked, "What in the world happened to that poor child's leg?" The teacher replied with three words: "I don't know." Here was this student, who, as it happened, had been in an automobile accident and broken his leg in several places, and the teacher had not even bothered to ask what had happened to him. Her excuse was that he was bad before he had the cast, so the cast was irrelevant.

One of the most basic human needs is the need to feel important. Some children are blessed. Their parents and families make them feel valued and important every day. This is wonderful, and we are fortunate, as teachers, to have some of these students in our classrooms. However, there are students who do not come from such ideal settings. These students are fortunate, at least, when they are placed in the classrooms of effective teachers who know how to make them feel valued and important. But regardless of whether students are valued at home, it is vital to make all of them feel important in our classrooms and in our schools. As one effective teacher put it:

> "I make it a point to say hello to every student I see in the hallways every day. Whether they are former students, current students, or students who may never be in my classroom, I know that my smile is easy to give, it's free, it makes us both feel better, and, sadly, for some, it may be the only friendly greeting they receive that day."

The most effective teachers, of course, go far beyond simply greeting students. They actually get to know something about each student's hobbies, personal interests, and dreams. They know that by getting to know their students on a personal level, their students will be much more likely to connect with them.

Research shows that teachers value principals who show an interest in the teachers' lives outside of school (*Motivating and Inspiring Teachers*, Whitaker et al., Eye On Education, 2001). The students in our classrooms feel the same way. They need to know us, for us to know them, and to know that we genuinely care about them, not just as students, but as people.

Having knowledge of a student's background can work to our benefit or to our detriment, determined only by what we do with the information. The most effective teachers know how to use it to their benefit. They use what they know about a student's background to help them better understand the student. Additionally, they use the information to help them personalize their approach with the student both on an instructional and a personal level. Effective teachers who are aware of a student with a challenging background never use that knowledge as an excuse for letting the student off the hook or, worse yet, letting themselves off the hook by giving up on the student.

Any teacher can teach the valedictorian, and we should all enjoy our experiences with this type of student. However, our most satisfying and validating experiences come from teaching those students who need us the most—those who may never be valedictorians, but who just might survive because of us.

> *So get to know your students, and let them know you, too*
> *One day they will succeed in life, in part because of you!*

Part 4.
How to Maximize the Power of Praise

The most effective teachers agree that praise is one of the most powerful tools we can use to positively impact our students. However, many teachers are unfamiliar with the effective use of praise. To simplify, just think of the word *success*:

> **S**—Specific
>
> **U**—Unconditional
>
> **C**—Credible
>
> **C**—Consistent
>
> **E**—Enthusiastic
>
> **S**—Stand Alone
>
> **S**—Suitable

Now let's take them one by one:

Being *specific* can greatly enhance the power of praise. Whatever behavior you reward is the one most likely to be repeated! So be specific about whatever behavior you want to see repeated. If you compliment a student on a nice sweater, you'll be amazed at the frequency with which he begins to wear that sweater. If you give a student attention only when he misbehaves, then you guarantee that the misbehavior will become more frequent. However, instead of noticing only the times he's talking and pointing that out, if you start noticing the times he's *not* talking and praising that behavior, you've just turned the situation around. By continually praising specific positive behaviors, you increase the likelihood that these behaviors will continue.

One of the most challenging aspects of praise is that it must be *unconditional*. It must be given as a gift without a return expected. The best teachers know this. They never expect anything in return for the praise they give to their students. But notice that you will often hear less effective teachers saying that praise does not work. That's because they are waiting for their return reward, in an implied trade-off: "I will be nice to you *only* if you'll be nice to me." This guarantees a power struggle, which is not what praise is all about.

Praise, at all times, must be *credible*. In order for a student to believe us, the praise should be true and genuine. Let's look at a real-life example to which most of us can relate—the oh-so-dreaded D word—*diet!* Though diets are difficult to adhere to, one of the best motivators is when people say to us, "You look great!" Isn't that a better motivator than someone saying to you, "It's about time!"?

Praise must also occur on a *consistent* basis. Think about this: It's not necessary to wait until someone loses 35 pounds before you compliment them. It works best if you compliment them the first time you catch them not "super-sizing" their fast-food meal! The same holds true in the classroom. The best teachers do not wait until students finish an entire task before they praise them. They know that praising the ongoing effort will serve to reinforce and enhance the finished product. Please understand that praising consistently does not mean we have to reinforce something every time it happens, but that we must do so on a regular, ongoing basis. As one effective teacher put it: "Students like to be praised for their actions, and they never get tired of it as long as it's authentic."

Praise should also be delivered in an *enthusiastic* manner. Making sure that the student is aware that you are pleased, proud, and so forth is important to the effectiveness of the praise. Ralph Waldo Emerson stated it best when he said, "Nothing great was ever achieved without enthusiasm."

Another critical aspect of praise is that it must *stand alone*. If we say something like, "You did a nice job on your reading quiz today, *but* on your math…" then the student hears nothing that comes before the word *but* and everything after! If someone were to ask you, "Have you been on a diet? You really look like you've lost weight, but what happened to your hair?" then you would most likely walk away feeling highly insulted by the insult instead of feeling pleased about the praise!

Finally, praise must be *suitable* to the particular student's situation. A student who struggles to accomplish anything may need to be praised for a simple attempt. This is appropriate for that particular student. On the other hand, praising a high achiever for a simple attempt is not appropriate. A student who never turns in homework needs to be praised if he or she finally turns it in once!

The fact is that treating students (who are not equal in their abilities and accomplishments) equally is inherently unfair. The same standard applies when using praise. However, please do not let the talent of a particular student deter you from praising. All students (and all adults!) appreciate being praised regardless of their ability levels.

Remember the word *success*. Each of the seven components is essential to the success of the praise:

S—Specific

U—Unconditional

C—Credible

C—Consistent

E—Enthusiastic

S—Stand Alone

S—Suitable

Part 5.
How to Use Rewards Appropriately

There are long-standing debates in education as to the value of using rewards in the classroom. Rewards may consist of tangible things, such as candy, stickers, or certificates, or intangible things, such as praise or recognition. The best teachers know that **the real secret is not whether you use rewards in the classroom, but whether you use them** *effectively.* Less effective teachers say things like, "Well, I shouldn't have to reward my students to get them to do things they're supposed to do anyway!" or "I'm not about to bribe my students with candy!" or "They never do anything right anyway. How can I possibly reward them?" Again, the real issue is not the reward itself but how the reward is used.

Let's take a look at tangible rewards. They can be something as simple as a gold star to something as elaborate as a scholarship. Regardless, it's not just the extrinsic value that serves as the motivator. The value that we, as teachers, place on the student's actions that lead to the reward is at least as important as the actual reward.

Let's look at an example in one particular middle school:

To decrease the number of negative behaviors, the school came up with a recognition program called "The Quarterly Challenge." Four times a year, every quarter, those students who did not have any tardy marks, office referrals, overdue library books, and so on, were rewarded. Rewards varied each quarter. They consisted of things like pizza parties for one quarter or half a day off of school for another. The goal, of course, was to increase the positive behaviors of the students in the school. This approach produced positive results in some classrooms and negative results in others. Further analysis revealed that these results had everything to do with the approaches of the teachers and very little, if anything, to do with the students.

It was discovered that in the classrooms of the most effective teachers, the Quarterly Challenge was used, on a daily basis, as a positive motivator. Both the teachers and the students were excited and enthusiastic about the positive behaviors that were leading to the reward at the end of the quarter. Conversely, the less effective teachers were holding the Quarterly Challenge over the heads of their students by threatening them. They were engaging in power struggles with the students by saying things such as, "If you don't improve your behavior, you won't get to do the Quarterly Challenge!" or "None of you will make it to the Quarterly Challenge if you keep up this behavior." In these classrooms, students, in their attempts to regain some control in the ongoing power struggles with the teachers, were pretending not to care about the reward. These students also began picking on the few students who actually were doing what was expected of them, saying things like, "Oh, boy! You're going to make it to the Quarterly Challenge. Fun, fun!" Not surprisingly, the overall behaviors of the students in the classrooms of the less effective teachers were steadily becoming worse, not better. Thus, these teachers argued that the Quarterly Challenge was not working. Again, it had nothing to do with the reward and everything to do with the approach of the teachers.

There's no such thing as being too old to like receiving a reward for a job well done, but no one wants that reward to be linked to a negative approach. Let's summarize:

A negative approach to a positive reward can discount anything positive about the reward itself, thus leaving a bad taste in the mouth of the person who was doing something positive to begin with!

> *It's not just the reward that will help me to try hard*
> *It's your approach to it all that will help me stand or fall*
> *So praise my efforts, please; accentuate the good*
> *And I just might succeed 'cause you believed that I could!*

Part 6.
How to Motivate Unmotivated Students

Unmotivated students are unmotivated because they are just not motivated! Now, having clarified that, let's look at why the best teachers seem to have a secret way of motivating unmotivated students. Instead of trying to figure out the secret, we simply went to some of the very best teachers and asked them to share the secret. Uncannily (or maybe not), they all seemed to agree on the following:

- An unmotivated student is a student who does not feel successful.
- Students who don't feel successful need teachers who are willing to help them become successful.
- Students who experience success become motivated to do better and try harder.
- Students don't come to us automatically and intrinsically motivated.
- Motivating students is the teacher's job.
- Some students are easier to motivate than others.
- The most difficult students to motivate are the very ones who need us, their teachers, the most.

Now, having stated what these teachers recognize about unmotivated students, we'll share what they feel is the best way to motivate unmotivated students:

- Identify that the student is unmotivated. This is the easy part!
- Express a belief in the student and his ability to accomplish the task at hand.
- Teach the student at his level. That's the only way he will experience any kind of success.
- As soon as he experiences success, praise that success, and nudge him gently to the next level.

We then asked, "But what about those times when lots of students seem unmotivated?" Here's what one effective teacher had to say:

"When I look around and see those 'dull' looks, those 'blank' stares, I immediately do something different. I raise the level of my enthusiasm, I ask different kinds of questions, I change the activity if I think it will help, and I basically do everything but stand on my head to change the mood at that point. It's my job to motivate and inspire my students, so I work hard at it and do whatever it takes."

Another effective teacher shared the following:

"I often find that when my students are not motivated, it's because they just don't see the point in why we're doing what we're doing. That's a red flag to me that I've forgotten to make that oh-so-critical real-life connection. So I do just that—I make what I'm teaching relate to the real lives of my students—and suddenly they're motivated!"

We also interviewed some less-than-effective teachers and asked the same questions regarding motivation in the classroom. Again uncannily (or maybe not), they all seemed to agree to the following:

- Some students are just impossible to motivate.
- Unmotivated students don't want to be motivated.
- Unmotivated students are lazy.
- It's not my job to motivate them. My job is to teach the content.
- Some students just don't care.

Do you notice how unmotivated their answers seem? Do these seem like motivated teachers in whose classrooms you would want to place your own children? Is it any wonder the students are not motivated?

Let's hear from the students now. We asked students what made some teachers' classes more motivating than others. Here are a few of their comments:

- Twelfth grader: "If my teacher seems motivated, that motivates me. If my teacher seems bored with her own lesson, it's hard to feel motivated."
- First grader: "When my teacher says 'good job' it makes me feel good. And then I try really hard to make her happy."
- Fifth grader: "I like when the lesson is exciting and fun. It makes it easy to understand."
- Third grader: "I had a teacher last year who didn't smile at us. I think she was mad, but I don't know why. But my teacher this year smiles a lot and it makes me happy to come to school."
- Second grader: "I don't think I'm too good at reading but my teacher is helping me to get better."
- Tenth grader: "I can't stand when a teacher just lectures and we have to take all those notes. It's boring, and I usually just don't listen."

◆ Seventh grader: "One of my teachers tells us stories about her life. She teaches us all the book stuff, but she's a real person, too. I like that."

Teachers, what really matters is not so much what students walk away with in their hands, but how many sparks you ignite in their hearts. Students want inspiration more than they want stuff. The teacher, not the content, determines whether students walk away ignited or extinguished.

Jason was a seventh-grade student who had been retained three times. He said that he never liked school because he just wasn't any good at it—that was, he said, until he encountered Mrs. Thomas, his seventh-grade teacher. From the very first day, he felt inspired. He felt successful. He could hardly believe the feeling, as it was one he had never experienced in school. His grades soared, and he soon caught up with his classmates—so much so that the school decided to move him on to the ninth grade. The following is a quote from Jason: "Being in Mrs. Thomas's class was like a dream come true. She made learning fun, and she found some talents in me that no one else had ever noticed. Had I had Mrs. Thomas years ago, I would probably be in the right grade today. I'm not a failure. I guess I just needed to be inspired."

> Teachers, you can be just as effective with your students as Mrs. Thomas was with Jason. Light a spark in all the students you teach. Help them to believe that they can, and they will!

Part 7.
How to Maximize the Power of *You*

We began this chapter by having you reflect on your favorite and least favorite teachers. None of us recall what was on page 147 of the textbook or the second essay question on the midterm exam. We all recall, however, how we felt and how we were treated. This is the power of emotion, the power of influence, the power of teachers!

As teachers, how we feel about ourselves helps to determine how we treat our students. Teaching requires so much of our energy and emotion. We often have little time to catch our breath during a busy day at school and sometimes not even the opportunity to use the restroom! Teaching is demanding. No one said it would be easy. If someone did, someone lied. But we must never forget that we *choose* to be teachers. We choose to make a difference. We choose to call ourselves professionals. Therefore, we cannot have an off day. The reason is simple: There are students in our care.

The very best teachers are the ones who always appear happy, who never seem to have a bad day, who are never overheard griping, whining, and complaining, who truly seem to like every student they teach. Is it possible that they really have no problems, that the rest of us just came out on the short end of the stick? Hardly. The most effective teachers shared a secret with us: They sometimes just fake it! But even better than that, we asked the best teachers how they manage to stay so upbeat and positive, regardless of how draining and demanding teaching can be. Here are some of the tips they shared with us, in their own words:

- ◆ "I have learned that sometimes, if you just smile, not only will you feel better, but your students will never know that you're having a bad day."

- ◆ "My students need as many positive role models as they can get. I am committed to being one of those, and I surely won't accomplish that by being negative. So it's not an option for me to be negative."

- ◆ "I use exercise as a release. It always makes me feel better."

- ◆ "I keep a book of motivational quotes and poems nearby, and I pick it up whenever I need a lift."

- ◆ "When I'm feeling overwhelmed, I simply remind myself of just how much my students need me and of why I chose teaching in the first place."

- "I take it out on my husband! Just kidding…"
- "I have a folder with positive letters from parents and students, and whenever I'm having a bad day, I read a few of those."
- "I often remind myself that teachers don't have the luxury of having a bad day. Neither do brain surgeons, thank goodness!"

> Remember, teachers, that your influence is powerful. Be it positive or negative, it is lasting. You will live in the hearts of your students long after you are gone from this earth. Your influence is eternal!

Secret Seven—Chapter Summary

Regarding motivation and inspiration, remember the following:
- Your actions and your moods will set the daily tone for the class.
- Act excited and motivated every day. Fake it if you must!
- Find the good in every child.
- Make every student feel like your favorite student.
- SUCCESS helps determine the impact of praise.
- Find ways to help keep *yourself* motivated and inspired.
- Do whatever it takes to motivate and inspire your students.
- Your influence is lasting, so make it positive!
- Make every student feel special. They all are!
- Make every student successful. They all can be!

Conclusion

It is our sincere belief that all teachers do the best they can with what they know. And thus our purpose for writing this book—we wanted to share with *all* teachers the seven simple secrets of the most successful teachers. So now that you know them, simply go out and do them.

And remember, teachers, that each child is someone special, worthy of the best you have to give. Find that someone special inside of each. Teach them hard and love them well!

A Hero Lies in Wait

Sitting in every one of those desks is pure, unbridled potential

I must look for the tiniest spark of a clue, though it may seem inconsequential

And despite the behaviors that mask what's there, what's there is mine to reveal

I must look beyond and see inside to all they think and feel

What's inside of the quiet mind? A philosopher? A writer?

And what's inside the rebellious one? I'll never know if I fight her

Which one will be the doctor who may someday cure a disease?

And which will be the adventurer who will one day sail on the breeze?

And who will be the motherly one who cares for her children's needs?

Which will be the philanthropist helping through unselfish deeds?

Who will be the mechanic, the attorney, or the pilot?

Who will climb the rainbow in search of indigo and violet?

I have to remind myself each day, so emotions will not lead my mind astray

That inside of every student I teach, a hero lies in wait

And the way I treat each one today will help to mold that fate.

An Invitation for Your Comments

It has been our pleasure to share with you the seven simple secrets of the very best teachers. We eagerly invite your input, your suggestions, or any stories you may wish to share for our future writings. Please feel free to contact us:

Annette Breaux: abreaux@eyeoneducation.com

Todd Whitaker: twhitaker@eyeoneducation.com

If you liked this book, we recommend:

101 "Answers" for New Teachers and Their Mentors:
Effective Teaching Tips for Daily Classroom Use
Annette L. Breaux

"There is no one I can recommend more highly than Annette Breaux."

Harry K. Wong, Author of
The First Days of School

This best selling book:
- generates instant impact on teaching and learning
- supports and sustains master classroom teachers who need help mastering their roles as mentors
- stimulates and organizes interactive sessions between new teachers and their mentors
- provides a collection of "thought provokers" and teaching tips for new teachers
- offers common sense strategies for any teacher seeking to be more effective

Topics include:
- Classroom Management
- Discipline
- Relating Lessons to Real Life
- Encouraging Active Student Participation
- Planning
- Professionalism, Attitudes and Behaviors of Effective Teachers

2003 180 pp. paperback 1-930556-48-9 $29.95

REAL Teachers, REAL Challenges, REAL Solutions:

25 Ways to Handle the Challenges of the Classroom Effectively

Annette and Elizabeth Breaux

"After reading this book, your teaching will never be the same. It is a must read for all teachers."

Harry K. Wong, Author of
The First Days of School

For new teacher induction programs or high-interest staff development workshops, this book helps new teachers—and experienced ones—find solutions to common classroom challenges. It shows teachers how to get students to do what they want them to do, deal with parents and difficult co-workers, and solve other common teaching challenges.

It presents 25 real scenarios along with "What's Effective," "What's NOT Effective," and "Bottom Line" strategies for handling teacher challenges.

2004, 120 pp. paperback 1-930556-64-0 $24.95

What Great Teachers Do *Differently*:
14 Things That Matter Most
Todd Whitaker

"This book is easy to read and provides essential information. I've ordered copies for every one of my teachers."

Anne Ferrell, *Principal*
Autrey Hill Middle School
Alpharetta, Georgia

This # 1 best selling book has been widely adopted in study groups and professional development programs across the country. It describes the beliefs, behaviors, attitudes, and interactions that form the fabric of life in our best classrooms and schools. It focuses on the specific things that great teachers do...that others do not.

It answers these essential questions—

- Is it high expectations for students that matter?
- How do great teachers respond when students misbehave?
- Do great teachers filter differently than their peers?
- How do the best teachers approach standardized testing?
- How can your teachers gain the same advantages?

2004, 144 pp. paperback 1-930556-69-1 $29.95

Great Quotes for Great Educators
Todd Whitaker and Dale Lumpa

Over 600 insightful, witty nuggets to motivate and inspire you...
...and everyone else at your school.

Teachers—display these quotes in your classrooms!

Administrators—insert them into your faculty memos and share them at staff meetings!

Why is this book *unique?*

◆ includes over 100 original quotes from internationally acclaimed speaker and educator Todd Whitaker

◆ features real quotes from real students, which echo wit and wisdom for educators

◆ each quote has a direct connection to your life as an educator

Examples of quotes in this book...

"Great teachers have high expectations for their students, but higher expectations for themselves."

Todd Whitaker

"We can never control a classroom until we control ourselves."

Todd Whitaker

2004, 208 pp. paperback 1-903556-82-9 $29.95 plus shipping and handling

Dealing with Difficult Parents
(And with Parents in Difficult Situations)
Todd Whitaker & Douglas J. Fiore

"This book is an easy read with common sense appeal. The authors are not afraid to share their own vulnerability and often demonstrate a sense of humor."

Gale Hulme, Program Director
Georgia's Leadership Institute
for School Improvement

This book helps teachers, principals, and other educators develop skills in working with the most difficult parents in the most challenging situations. It shows you how to:

- ◆ avoid the "trigger" words that serve only to make bad situations worse.
- ◆ use the right words and phrases to help you develop more positive relationships with parents.
- ◆ deal with parents who accuse you of not being fair.
- ◆ build positive relationships with even the most challenging parents.

2001, 175 pp. paperback 1-930556-09-8 $29.95 plus shipping and handling

Teaching Matters:
Motivating & Inspiring Yourself
Todd and Beth Whitaker

"This book makes you want to be the best teacher you can be."

Nancy Fahnstock
Godby High School
Tallahassee, Florida

Celebrate the teaching life! This book helps teachers:

- rekindle the excitement of the first day of school all year long
- approach every day in a "Thank God it is Monday" frame of mind
- not let negative people ruin your day
- fall in love with teaching all over again

Brief Contents

- Why You're Worth it
- Unexpected Happiness
- Could I Have a Refill Please? (Opportunities for Renewal)
- Celebrating Yourself
- Raise the Praise–Minimize the Criticize
- Making School Work for You

2002, 150 pp. paperback 1-930556-35-7 $24.95 plus shipping and handling